Honest Surrender
holding nothing back

Angelie Patsianis

Ark House Press
PO Box 1722, Port Orchard, WA 98366 USA
PO Box 1321, Mona Vale NSW 1660 Australia
PO Box 318 334, West Harbour, Auckland 0661 New Zealand
arkhousepress.com

© Angelie Patsianis 2021

Unless otherwise stated, all Scriptures are taken from the New Living Translation (Holy Bible. New Living Translation copyright© 1996, 2004, 2007, 2013 by Tyndale House Foundation. Used by permission of Tyndale House Publishers Inc., Carol Stream, Illinois 60188. All rights reserved.)

Some names and identifying details have been changed to protect the privacy of individuals.

Cataloguing in Publication Data:
Title: Honest Surrender
ISBN: 978-0-6450375-8-6 (pbk)
Other Authors/Contributors: Patsianis, Angelie

Cover designed by Alexi Patsianis
Interior designed by initiateagency.com

CONTENTS

ONE: Out Of Hiding (Steffany Gretzinger) 1

TWO: Letting Go (Steffany Gretzinger) 16

THREE: Defender (Upper Room) 33

FOUR: Touch Of Heaven (Hillsong Worship) 48

FIVE: Father's Love (Futures Worship) 60

SIX: Even When It Hurts (Hillsong Worship) 74

SEVEN: Be Okay (Zoe Worship) 82

EIGHT: Lean Back (Capital City feat. Dion Davis) 93

NINE: Heart Of God (Hillsong Young And Free) 102

TEN: To Worship You I Live (Israel Houghton) 116

ELEVEN: Grace To Grace (Hillsong Worship) 127

Bible Scripture References 137

About The Author 139

ACKNOWLEDGMENTS

To my incredible husband Alexi, who has patiently journeyed with me throughout this entire process. Thank you for speaking life into me, believing in me and for your constant support. I adore you.

To my baby sis Kym, who has walked with me every step of the way. Thank you for your consistent love and support. You inspire me more than you'll ever know.

To my Publisher and Editor at Ark House Press. Thank you for listening to my testimony and catching the vision from the beginning. You have turned the manuscript into a book that is so full of life.

To one of my most trusted friends, Beth. Thank you for taking the time to assist me with improving its overall content flow. Your encouragement means the world to me.

My heart is overwhelmed with so much gratitude for my family, friends and leaders who have made such a huge impact on my life. I wouldn't be the woman I am today if it weren't for your guidance and love. Thank you for championing and empowering me to become bold towards the things of God and my pursuit in Him.

To our Heavenly Father, I put nothing else above you and choose to honour you with my whole life.

ANGELIE PATSIANIS

INTRODUCTION

I wasn't ever sure where to start when it came to writing a book. I always found the concept of having my own book published quite intimidating. On the contrary, I was prophesied over more than once that I would write one, but I always seemed to shrug off the idea because I didn't think I was capable enough. Yet here we are, with God surprising me in more ways than I could imagine. Isn't it funny how even after we think we've got Him all figured out, He still surprises us with the new ideas and works He prompts us to do? Questioning, debating, challenging and then eventually surrendering and trusting Him, sometimes with no real understanding or clue where to go next. As I become older, I'm continuously learning to be content with the mystery and giving over control to Him. I've learnt to take these steps of faith, listen to The Holy Spirit and be open to where I'm led to next. There's always something new to learn and I've come to realise that allowing God to take the reigns of our life actually leads us to better places anyway. So why not just take part in His adventure and experience all the goodness He has to offer? I'm not saying it'll always be easy, because we all know there are times we struggle to obey. But throughout my life, I've experienced that every time I've made an intentional decision to surrender myself to God, I've found that what follows never disappoints.

At the start of the book, you may have noticed that each chapter has been titled with the name of a song. In some way along my walk with God, each song has been able to speak to me through their God-given lyrics. Music can be such a powerful tool during a trial to help us realign our hearts to Him and it wasn't just the words where I felt a depth of connection with my Heavenly Father, but it was the reassurance of His love, His immense peace and His overall presence that was so evident in those moments of listening to these songs, as I spent time with Him. It was these particular worship songs chosen for each chapter that represent what I feel God's heart was wanting to remind me during those seasons of my life.

I'm no Bible scholar or theologian; I'm simply someone who has experienced too much of God's goodness in my life that it was impossible to keep it all to myself. As you read on, I'll be sharing my story on how God reintroduced me to honest surrender through His continuous grace and how I was healed from my past through God's restoration, even when I felt less than deserving of His attention. I also detail how He journeyed me through a long-term relationship ending in order for me to fall back in love with Jesus. He mended my relationship with Him and showed me the posture of honest surrender before restoring that same long-term relationship with my husband, Alexi. Lastly, I will be sharing about how He transformed seasons of absolute gut-wrenching heartache into a reminder of His overwhelming grace and renewing confidence in Him.

In whatever season you're in, I hope this book encourages you to place God at the centre of your world; taking your surrender to deeper places in Him. I pray that God reveals Himself to you in every chapter and that you are drawn closer in relationship with Him. It may not always be easy to choose surrender, especially when there are many things in life that can come out from left, right and centre to distract us. However, the more we learn to actively choose to drop our own defences, lay down our ways of control and really lean in to trust in His precious ways, the more we will truly see that He in fact has more for our lives than we could ever imagine. With the more that God has, He desires to bless us in every aspect of our life, even in the mundane.

At times, we can get so caught up in our own pain and it can be incredibly overwhelming to really comprehend the bigger picture, but one of the wonderful things about God is that He always turns what the enemy meant for harm for our good and for His glory.

Genesis 50:20 AMP
As for you, you meant evil against me, but God meant it for good in order to bring about this present outcome, that many people would be kept alive [as they are this day].

I'm just one of many people who are a living testimony of making it through one of my tough seasons by choosing God's path and as a result, seeing His goodness and experiencing His victory. Like all of us, there are still things that I'm learning along the way, but through these experiences, I am now able to boldly declare God's goodness through the power of my testimony and how freeing it is to do so. There are millions of people in the world who have experienced God's love, mercy and grace, just as I have, but what a humbling experience it is to be able to share a portion of my story with you… something so raw and personal. My prayer is for you to also experience that same pursuing love, mercy and grace in all the ways God is desiring to show you, as you choose the ways of honest surrender.

ONE

Out Of Hiding

I once heard that the font 'Comic Sans' speeds up the writing process and sparks creativity. I remember seeing it on a Facebook post prior to writing this book and recall thinking to myself, "I'll suss it out and see if it actually works." This book obviously isn't published in Comic Sans font, however I did use it while writing the draft and to my surprise, it really does help! I can confidently say that Comic Sans is very useful with getting those creative juices flowing in the mind. I don't know how, but I'm glad I discovered it. Right now, you're probably thinking to yourself, *What is the purpose of you telling me this?* Well, similar to me trying out Comic Sans to help me with my book writing skills (odd comparison I know), if you're reading this book with the intention of 'sussing it out', I truly hope that it reveals or even simply reminds you that choosing God's way actually works. I don't know the mysteries behind how He works things out for our good; all I know is that He does it better than we ever could.

If you're anything like me, chapter one is always my favourite part of any book because when I start reading, I get so consumed and by this point, it feels like I'm about to enter into a whole new world. I always get excited, anticipation takes place and I'm filled with an array of emotions. It prepares me to learn and take in the thoughts, perspectives and experiences of other people in their journey of life with God. Most of my own personal experiences have been learnt from past mistakes, God revealing His grace and from people who have walked the journey before me. This has confirmed that there is a vast difference between giving God control and giving ourselves control. Surrendering to God brings about His peace and His freedom, that cannot be experienced or found elsewhere.

Philippians 4:7 AMP
And the peace of God [that peace which reassures the heart, that peace] which transcends all understanding, [that peace which] stands guard over your hearts and your minds in Christ Jesus [is yours].

HONEST SURRENDER

John 8:36 AMP
So if the Son makes you free, then you are unquestionably free.

So, where do I even begin? I wrestled back and forth with the idea of writing a book. I knew that it was something God was encouraging me to do and The Holy Spirit was gentle and patient with His prompts, but I just didn't think I was qualified enough to even write one. I had thoughts like: "Who would even read it?" "Who am I to even write a book?" "You ain't no Francine Rivers guuuuurl". When I actually decided to start writing, I felt a spur of excitement. It was empowering to know that it wasn't just me behind this idea, but it was God breathing vision into life. He was the reason why I even had this unexplainable courage to begin with. He saw things in me that I wasn't capable of spotting out for myself, or just straight out avoided. However, all of this stemmed from a revelation of completely surrendering myself to Him and it all developed through opportunities of growth that God allowed in my life to take place. Sometimes the opportunities can be difficult to achieve, but it is in those trying moments where God is able to reveal His complete goodness and glory to us. Sometimes we can so easily desire to rush to the end, to avoid enduring the labour and the pain, but it's in the process of the stumbling where we are able to fully appreciate His guidance of being picked back up; where we are able to fully experience the Truth of who He is,

His sovereignty, faithfulness and unconditional love. The peace that follows after, or even in the midst of the countless falls, is never short of remarkable. It's what helps to keep us grounded and found in Him.

Growing up and learning to venture through life as a young girl, while transitioning to become a woman in this high-expected-society (not to mention trying to let go of specific past attachments in the midst of it all), wasn't as simple as I anticipated it to be. I had always been naturally one to like feeling in control of my life and my surroundings. I'm structured, organised and I usually want to know what's ahead of time. I like when things are planned out and having an idea of what's to come. Before allowing God to be involved in any of my life plans, I had become too independent, too self-driven and the worst part about it was, I didn't even realise how selfish in my own thinking I had become. God, on the other hand, needed me to become more dependent on Him in order for me to truly grasp and appreciate what He had in store for me. I had to learn the hard way by taking the difficult path, but isn't that always the best way to learn? Well, at least for me, learning the hard way was exactly what I needed.

Rewinding back to where it all began, I was born in the Philippines and moved to Adelaide, South Australia when I was around six months old. Although I grew up in a westernised culture, my parents still incorporated Filipino culture into the household. Needless to say, it was mixed with all sorts of fun and chaos. I grew up in a home that was loud and opinionated. The mix of personalities felt like we were living in a reality TV show and everyone contributed to the madness.

Firstly, you have my Mum, who is one of the most extroverted and EXTRA people you could ever meet. She is super-loud, hilarious, always has an opinion and she would argue about anything and everything, convinced that she was right ninety percent of the time. She was the real queen and diva of the household, yet always found ways to bring the family joy. Although she carried an opinion a majority of the time, I always admired her boldness and still to this day, I'm grateful for that confidence she taught us as children. Mum and I didn't have the best relationship growing up. In my early years of womanhood, we would fight on a consistent basis. Every day seemed like a living nightmare and to escape her wrath, I decided to move out with my boyfriend at the time. Later in life I learnt that this was an even worse decision.

After her separation with my Dad, I hated that there were different men coming in and out of the house, a place I was supposed to feel at home the most. I felt trapped. I had also convinced myself that she would never understand me as a person, but as I grew older, the relationship between us mended and by allowing forgiveness to take place in our hearts, it brought us closer. My Mum is kind, generous and has never stopped loving us. My younger self was blinded from seeing what I see now. I'm grateful for a praying mother who chose to spiritually fight for us as children and still to this day, continues to fight for us in spiritual warfare.

My Dad, on the other hand, was a little more reserved and timid. Although he was quieter, he became a little more talkative when he had the opportunity to share his 'dad jokes' and if you really caught him in a joker mood, the banter would carry on and there was no stopping it. When we were younger, Dad worked hard to provide for our family and I was always grateful for his example; working two to three jobs for the family, then coming home without complaint and still choosing to shower us with unconditional love. This was a strength I admired. Growing up, I was Daddy's girl. You'd find me cuddled up to him on the couch or wherever he was. I absolutely adored him. As I became older, our relationship grew sour because of the past and the pain behind my Dad hardly taking any responsibility for the divorce with my Mum. Over the years, I would feel so much anger towards him as he opened up to me about how he felt in the marriage, with every conversation being centred on him, while disregarding how it affected anybody else. I would wait for him to say, "I'm so sorry for the pain I've caused". I would long for him to ask about how

I was coping. I was convinced for a while that this was a question I would have to ask myself. I stayed silent and dealt with it on my own for a long time because I didn't feel like I had the voice to say how I really felt. I would be contacted by numerous women he was involved with, each one attempting to mother me and win my approval. During this time, resentment became one of my closest companions.

The day I found out I had two half sisters in the Philippines, broke me in two. I was told that my siblings and I would never meet one of them, because the mother of his daughter wanted nothing to do with my Dad. It took me some time to reach out to my other half sister, Nikka, but I'm so glad that I did. I now have a deep love for her and look forward to when we meet. At the time, there were no apologies for his actions, only complaints about how difficult life had been for him since the divorce. His victim mentality left me feeling emotionally wounded for a long while.

All I wanted to do in those moments was shout, "I'm hurting. We're all hurting. You're not the only one who has suffered. Do you ever think about how much this affects us too?" However, God always makes a way to come through. I have always believed that God brings restoration in lives and as I attempted to rebuild my relationship with Dad, I was able to see another prayer answered. It was on Father's Day, 2020 where God brought about the forgiveness I had been longing for. It was on the Sunday morning Father's Day church service where my Dad mentioned that he was touched by the message our Lead Pastor, Josh Greenwood, had shared. He spoke about how much our Heavenly Father loves us and the cost He was willing to sacrifice to see His children saved from condemnation. After the preach, my siblings and I took Dad out to lunch and it was there where he poured out to us, apologising for the hurt he had put us through. It was the first time I'd ever seen him lower his pride and take responsibility for his actions.

At that moment, I tried to keep myself together, like all the other times I was with him. However, this time around it felt different. Every bitter or grudge-bearing thought I had of my Dad was taken away and all I could feel for him was an overwhelming sense of love and forgiveness. Stored up hatred was removed in an instant and I knew that if it weren't for God, I would have responded in a completely different manner. God has truly taught me to look past those old hurts, to forgive him and move forward. I am now able to recognise Dad as the same sweet, caring and loving father I had always known as a child.

Then there were the children. My eldest sister always had more of a dominant personality and ever since she was little, my parents had mentioned many times how clever she was. I've always looked up to her natural intelligence. She could study for such a short amount of time and would still ace her exams on the day. She really was some sort of genius and I always wondered how she did it with such ease. Sometimes I would even spy on her while she studied to see what her secret to being so smart was, but there was no secret. She just had a naturally brilliant mind. When we were younger, all the siblings would try to avoid arguments with her because she always appeared to be right and you could never seem to win against her in one. We just settled with the fact that since she was so smart, she was probably right every time. She is also very strong mentally, as well as emotionally and has the mental capacity to fiercely fight through any challenges that come her way.

I watched as she and her husband fought to be where they are now, battling circumstances together that tried so hard to deter them. It's her resilience that played a huge part towards showing me that personal fears could be conquered and to this day, I'm inspired by the way she continues to carry herself, despite the uncertainties of life.

My older brother is the only boy of the siblings. He has always been so peaceful, patient and caring. Mum has always favoured him, maybe because he was the only boy. However, I'm more convinced that it was mostly because he reflected the heart of Christ so well. I always admired how he made decisions so firmly and chased after what he loved. He demonstrated this well as I watched how he pursued his wife. I now look at their marriage and I'm inspired by how they love one another. He was also very logical and balanced his sisters out when we would be too emotional in making decisions… Thank God for brothers.

Then there was me, the middle child (well close enough to it anyway). I was more of the mediator in the home. Whenever arguments would take place, I would always make it my duty to ensure that everyone was at peace with one another, although I didn't particularly enjoy confrontation. If you attacked my loved ones, the sassy and feisty side of me would come out. That was a side of me I tried to avoid. I was always very thankful for the close bond we had as siblings and although we grew up with disagreements, our parents brought us up to love and care for each other deeply.

Lastly is my youngest sister, who takes after my Mum and Dad as the diva and the joker. She was mischievous a majority of her childhood and the entertainment of the household, always making us laugh uncontrollably. Still to this day, she's one of the most entertaining and funniest people I know. She even owns a costume box for fun. She has dressed up as a lot of different things: an elf, the Grinch, a hobbit, an angel, a pineapple, a medieval knight… way too many characters to count off of one hand. She's an absolute character, I know, but she has this amazing ability to easily bring out the best in anyone, of any age. It's very admirable. Even though she's the baby of the family, I've always been inspired by her vulnerability. She chooses to trust God, even when life is constantly shifting and she continues to cling to Him, even when people have wounded her fragile heart. She loves others without limits and while there's every reason to throw the towel in and choose not to forgive a person, she continues to pour out what seems to be an endless supply of grace. She's someone who inspires me daily. All of my family do.

This is my family and you could imagine how the mix of personalities would've blended under one roof. It was a wonderful madness. Despite the ruckus that was in our home, my parents were actually raised as Catholics. I only have very vague memories of going to Mass and I was still a child when we converted to Christianity. Growing up, my parents weren't all perfect (who are we kidding, what parents are?) and although their marriage suffered along the way, I'll always be incredibly grateful for parents who chose for us as siblings to be planted in the ways of God. These Godly values and Biblical Truths have always stuck by me and they will remain imprinted on my heart, regardless of what may come my way.

I grew up in what you'd call nowadays a 'broken home', but it wasn't always broken. I remember my Mum and Dad really loving each other throughout some of my childhood years. Even though I have memories of them arguing, quarrelling, fighting and yelling, I still recall feeling generally happy and loved as a child. It wasn't until I was in my senior year where things started to really hit the fan and my life took a turn for what I defined as my kind of worst. When I took the focus off myself, I started to realise that the relationship between my parents was quite rocky. I remember finding out that they were going to separate, eventually heading towards a divorce and during that time, not knowing how to feel. I knew that my Dad had been unfaithful to my Mum and my Dad had felt belittled by her throughout the marriage, but I didn't realise how much bitterness and rage had developed between them. It was a vicious cycle of blaming one another for the wrongs they had made, but somehow I convinced myself that despite those sore emotions, they would still work it all out, fight it through and stay together.

I was very wrong. At the time of their separation, I wasn't sad, neither was I angry; I just felt completely numb. There was no emotion attached to it and I honestly thought that was the right way to feel about it all. I continued going to school emotionless towards my parent's decision and since everyone else's parents were separated, I reasoned with myself to believe that it was just a typical part of life. But there is nothing normal about a divorce; it's a tactic from the enemy to destroy families. He carries the false claim that divorces are part of the norm. Marriage is a reflection of what God's relationship with the church is supposed to look like. It's a commitment, a covenant and the importance of this sacred bond and unity should always be fought for.

Ephesians 5:25 AMP
Husbands, love your wives, just as Christ loved the church and gave himself up for her.

1 Corinthians 7:10 NIV
To the married I give this command (not I, but the Lord): A wife must not separate from her husband. But if she does, she must remain unmarried or else be reconciled to her husband. And a husband must not divorce his wife.

At the time, I was so oblivious and just plain ignorant towards taking interest in my personal responses. The unfaithfulness on my Dad's end was extremely difficult to deal with and the arguments around it had left me feeling emotionally paralysed and lifeless. How would I have known that the traumas and experiences from my childhood would follow my decisions into the years that followed? In a time where I should have paid more attention to my decisions, I chose to rebel against what seemed good. Little did I know, it was the choices I made from where I was onwards that played a large role towards who I was becoming.

I have never personally experienced a divorce and I could only imagine how difficult and heart wrenching it would be to go through with one. I do know, though, how it feels to grow up feeling like you had to choose one or the other parent. Although the divorce itself wasn't my fault, I understand how it feels to carry the guilt, shame and weight of it all and feeling as if you're somehow responsible for it or that you could have done something to prevent it from even happening. The older I grew, the more the divorce and separation affected me and I realised that the underlying root issues had not been dealt with.

Having the natural qualities of a mediator, I remember going to visit my Dad on weekends and feeling as if I needed to create peace between him and my Mum. I wanted to make sure that on both ends they had at least forgiven each other, so there was some sort of avenue for them to work things out. As I grew older, I finally accepted that they weren't ever going to become remarried, but the older I became, the more I feared for my own life and my future family one day. I didn't want to ever experience divorce and because of my Dad's unfaithfulness to my Mum, I held a deep fear that my husband would be unfaithful to me too. These dreadful thoughts loomed over me because it was all I ever knew about 'family'. It became a fear that had attempted to make a home in me. I even entertained that fear, giving it a couch to sit on, some cushions to keep it comfy and probably even an ottoman to have it rest its feet up on. I lingered on that fear for a very long time.

It wasn't until I became a woman that I made a decision for deliverance to take place, but as a young adult experiencing what I had as a result of the family tension, I settled with the lie of the enemy that it was inevitable for something bad to happen to my own family one day. That was the enemy's way of getting a hold of my mind, constantly reminding me that I wasn't good enough, that I always needed to prove myself worthy of being loved, whether that was to a friend, a boy, a family member, a colleague, or any type of relationship. However, we don't have to prove ourselves to be worthy, because Jesus died on the cross for us all, to show us that we are in fact already worthy of His love and affection.

Romans 5:8 NIV
But God demonstrates his own love for us in this: While we were still sinners, Christ died for us.

TWO

Letting Go

In year twelve, my final year of school, I was convinced I was living my best life. I had good friends and followed life's rules well. I was in and out of my commitment to God, but in my mind I felt as if I wasn't doing anything wrong and therefore, I was sure to be in God's good books, even though I know now that there is no such thing.

I didn't particularly like showing emotion to my family and found it embarrassing to cry or show any sort of 'weakness' to them, but since my parents were processing their divorce, it gave me the perfect opportunity to train myself to keep my emotions hidden. At the time, it seemed like the best way to deal with them… or so I thought. During that period of time, I had learnt to suppress those emotions well and decided to concentrate on 'me and my life', with selfish desires, self-gratitude and self pleasures clouding my mind. Looking back, I realise how self consumed I was and how destructive I had become internally. I was selfish in the way I made decisions and manipulated situations, but at the time, all I thought about was fulfilling my needs.

As a young girl, I needed some sort of an outlet to escape my family problems. I needed an excuse to get away. I despised being around my parents at the time and hated how their actions made me feel. That's when I turned to boys, a dangerous place to be when you're already so caught up in life and emotionally vulnerable to what the world has to offer. I had a crush on a couple of guys and some of those crushes actually turned into my boyfriends. None of them were serious, of course. My young self so innocently gave in to their charm just to make me feel some kind of emotion again. Maybe you can relate to this selfishness, where you only thought of yourself and didn't stop to consider how it would affect you in the long run. For me, I never really considered how Jesus would have felt when I chose to make a reckless decision and yet even when we fail to consider how Jesus would feel, He still chooses to love and accept us anyway, never allowing anything to stand in the way of that love.

The moment I thought I had my first real, serious boyfriend was also the very moment I gave the enemy an opportunity to corrupt my mind. This took a turn for the worse and it affected me deeply. Due to my broken family past, I already had a distorted view of love and would try to find ways towards filling the void in my heart. This toxic relationship was an attempt of trying to fill that void. Convincing my young self that this was real love, I found myself in a physically and emotionally abusive relationship for four years. At seventeen, I lost my virginity and I remember feeling like a part of me had been torn and ripped into shreds. I had always imagined my first time to feel pure and beautiful and even grew up learning the Biblical Truth that God's creation of sex is intended for marriage. I would hear it all through my youth group and sermons in church, as well as my Mum, who constantly reminded me. Now don't get me wrong; if that's a choice that was made out of marriage, there is always grace and forgiveness for every past decision we've made. Our Father never holds any type of sin against us and we are loved regardless of our past. Back then, it was unhealthy for me to beat myself up over and over again for that one choice because despite the act, God still loved me and saw me as His child, just as He would with anyone else who falls into sin.

At seventeen, I was exposed to pornography and I acted like I was okay with all these sudden changes and expectations, but inside, I was rotting away. I was confused, attached, bound and no longer the good girl everyone perceived me to be. I had always wanted to set a good example for my younger sister, Kym, but after my reckless decisions, I felt like I had let her down too. I felt untrue to myself and to God, yet like any other addiction, I clung to this boy as my only means of assurance. As a young woman, I was so ashamed to have been exposed to this darker side, yet the longer I stayed in this destructive and toxic relationship, the more weight and tied down I felt. It was as if I was enslaved and couldn't leave him, even if I wanted to.

In our later years of dating, I was physically abused for situations that I would be blamed for and even after experiencing the internal and external pain, I was still somehow convinced that this was the level of happiness I deserved. When I felt extremely down, I gave in to the lie that it was the best I could ever receive. My parents started to notice the bruises from my abusive relationship and my close friends and family would warn me that it wasn't safe to go down this dark path, yet in my reluctance and self reliance, I continued to give in to the enemy and his lies. At the time of that relationship, I felt like I needed to stay with him to sustain that happiness and I found that I was only tolerating him, rather than actually experiencing love. I battled within myself and stuck around in fear of not being able to find anything better.

I felt trapped, stuck and completely alone. But despite how I felt, God stayed by my side, waiting for me to reach out to Him, longing for my response. He would prompt me through my pastors and supportive friends who never stopped loving me and amidst all the darkness, I would feel a soft tugging within. In every low moment, God was right there, patiently waiting for me to come back to Him. That's just the nature of who He is: kind, loving, patient and forgiving. Like in the story of The Prodigal Son, our Heavenly Father is waiting for His child to return to Him with open arms and that's exactly what He was like with me.

Luke 15:20 NIV
But while he was still a long way off, his father saw him and was filled with compassion for him; he ran to his son, threw his arms around him and kissed him.

I realised that because I had experienced a false idea of love from my seventeen year-old failed relationship, it put me off from dreaming big; dreaming of what it would be like to get married, becoming a wife and being a mother. I thought that maybe down the track it could happen, but was never really certain or confident in it and so decisions I made along the way didn't fully reflect how I saw myself in the future. All of this started to change when my ex-boyfriend decided to break up with me for good. I tried so hard to make things work and we went back and forth for a while, but I knew it was the right thing to let it go. At the time, enduring the pain of a break up absolutely killed me, but in hindsight, it was actually one of the best decisions I could have ever made. In the healing process, I turned to God and allowed Him to work inside of me. It became a regular part of life to desire the pursuit of Godliness. It was from this change on where I properly met my husband, Alexi, who was only an acquaintance at the time of my previous relationship, but in the years to come, became a very close friend of mine.

Regardless of what I thought about myself and my future, God's patience never gave up. Even though I took my time making reckless decisions, He still saw me as worth waiting on and that's exactly the same view He has with all of us. He doesn't see the terrible parts that we only want to see in ourselves. He actively *chooses* to see us as a whole. Despite how we view ourselves, whether that be as blemished, scarred, torn or scattered, He disregards all of that, redefines the distorted image we paint of ourselves and sees us as pure, loved, worthy and restored; we are as His most prized possession.

2 Corinthians 5:17 AMP
Therefore if anyone is in Christ [that is, grafted in, joined to Him by faith in Him as Savior], he is a new creature [reborn and renewed by the Holy Spirit]; the old things [the previous moral and spiritual condition] have passed away. Behold, new things have come [because spiritual awakening brings a new life].

Deuteronomy 26:18 NIV
And the Lord has declared this day that you are his people, his treasured possession as he promised, and that you are to keep all his commands.

One thing that Satan revels in is when we keep things hidden. In fact, he thrives off of it. Looking back on how I responded to hardships, I now realise that being honest and open with ourselves and God is what helps us deal with the struggles and hurts we face, more than we realise. Struggles, addictions and sin, which have been kept in secret, have the ability to eat away at us if it's not brought into the light, ultimately making us feel trapped and creating the false belief that we aren't able to escape it. It's God's desire for us to come out of hiding and to bring what was once in darkness into the light. By bringing our secret sin into the light, we are actually destroying the power it has in our lives.

Ephesians 5:11-14 AMP
Do not participate in the worthless and unproductive deeds of darkness, but instead expose them [by exemplifying personal integrity, moral courage, and godly character]; for it is disgraceful even to mention the things that such people practice in secret. But all things become visible when they are exposed by the light [of God's precepts], for it is light that makes everything visible. For this reason He says, "Awake, sleeper, And arise from the dead, And Christ will shine [as dawn] upon you and give you light."

This concept was something I struggled with for a long time because when it came to the past sin I committed, I was so ashamed by what I had done and what I believed I had become. I made the mistake of keeping it all to myself, causing me to spiral down into a dark hole. It was only until I made the decision to repent of what I had done and was genuinely wanting to take serious steps towards change that began my journey in finding liberation through Christ. At the time, I never really liked the idea of being 'accountable', but I knew in order for me to take the change seriously, I had to step out of my own comfort zone and confide in Godly leaders I knew were trustworthy. Like the title of this chapter suggests, I needed to *let go* of old habits, ways of thinking and pride towards thinking I knew any better. Exposing the sin in itself was incredibly freeing, but it was now a journey of surrendering to Him on a daily basis that I needed to continue to learn and grow in so that I could live out the freedom He had wanted for me all along. I felt safe knowing God was with me and the same can be for you.

What does surrendering mean to us? I took the time to ask a few people what surrender (in a God-given context) meant to them and below are the responses that vary from different age groups, both male and female. These answers were gathered from close friends, prominent church leaders and family:

Chris, 63 - *"God has a plan for our lives, and to SURRENDER to Him means we lay aside our own plans, and we seek His will and purpose first, every day. The good news is that God's plan for us is always the very best, unlike our own plans!" (Jeremiah 29:11, "For I know the plans I have for you," declares the Lord, "plans to prosper you and not to harm you, plans to give you hope and a future." NIV.)*

Akuol, 25 - *"Surrender means giving all control to God, even when we don't understand."*

HONEST SURRENDER

Natasha, 18 - *"Honest surrender to me, is giving your all to God even when you're at the lowest point of your life or in a challenging season. Fully believing and knowing that He is in control and handing it all over to Him, so that you don't carry the burden. It can be shown physically by truly worshipping him or in your daily lives with the actions you use. It looks different to everyone and it is between you and God."*

Nazra, 57 - *"Surrender to me means to give up complete control of something to someone. To give up completely and to let go. The Christian believer completely gives up his or her will to God."*

Gillean, 30 - *"When I think of surrender I simply think: 'not my will but His.' I think to let go of control and to give God complete control over my life (future, thoughts, plans and more)."*

Kelly, 36 - *"Two definitions of 'Surrender,' according to the Noah Webster dictionary of 1828, are as follows:*
1. To yield to the power of another; to give or deliver up possession upon compulsion or demand.
2. To yield; to give up; to resign in favor of another; as, to surrender a right or privilege; to surrender a place or an office.

The very essence of being a born again believer in Jesus Christ is this idea of surrender: completely giving up control of my life, laying down my will on the altar in total sacrifice in order to gain that which is priceless: a full-access, intimate relationship with the Spirit of God. We can spend many years fighting to maintain control of our lives, but it is always in full surrender to God that we find our true identities, our true purpose, our true selves, and a fulfilled existence walking hand in hand with the Father. Apart from yielding to His will, we will make countless mistakes and often completely miss our true calling, but the great paradox is that when we relinquish control, we gain the beautiful freedom God created for us in the Garden of Eden. When I give up the right to myself, I gain the right to approach God's very throne, and therefore gain access to everything that is His. Surrender is often done in tears, but the benefits are reaped with joy. Full surrender can be terrifying, but God is asking you now if you would dare to see the beauty on the other side of the curtain. Will you dare to relinquish your right to yourself in order to gain the Kingdom of Heaven? Those who have done so will tell you themselves that it isn't easy, but the rewards are exponentially greater than staying safely in control. It's the greatest invitation you'll ever receive."

HONEST SURRENDER

One common response that I noticed in every person's answer was letting go of our own control and allowing God to take the lead. I'm assuming that nobody likes the idea of being controlled or being told what to do, but in this instance, I believe the idea of God being 'in control' can sometimes be misunderstood. For some, God is seen as this big, bad guy out to tell us how to live our lives. Not to mention, He can be looked upon as someone who wants to make our lives boring and uninteresting, but that couldn't be further from the truth. People tend to forget the fact that God has still given us free choice in life.

Personally, the choices I make aren't because I'm forced to make them, but they're made because I've been able to recognise how much He truly loves me and the extent of what He's saved me from. This in turn has caused my response to *want* to surrender to His will. Through these convictions, I have realised that if I'm in control of my own life, experiencing peace in my heart, mind and soul will always be something I'll struggle to fight for, where as with God guiding me, He offers His peace, freely and willingly.

We live in a society that is governed under rules and regulations, as well as having particular laws put in place so that people are accountable to their actions. Imagine living in a world where there were no rules and no consequences for what we did? If you've seen the American movie 'The Purge', you would have a visual idea of how chaotic life would be. Laws provide general protection and safety for the people living within them. If somebody commits a crime, they are destined to suffer the correct consequences for their wrongdoing. If this is all part of the physical world we live in, then why does it all of a sudden become an issue when we apply it to the spiritual world? In the same way that as human beings, we have freedom of speech and are able to make our own choices in life, yet are governed by laws to protect us (as well as to help us live in peace and avoid anarchy), is a similar way to how God desires us to live according to His Truth.

This is not with the intention to control us, but for us to simply live a life of protection and complete freedom, where we are able to fulfill the greater purposes He has for us. It's essential that we still have the freedom in making our own choices, but by allowing God's guidance in the decisions we make, it actually brings about much more freedom than we realise. Similar to laws providing a sense of general protection and safety for the people living within them, is the same way our Father wants to be our constant protector and safety net for our lives.

For some people, 'surrender' can come across as having negative connotations, such as giving up, failure and losing victory, but that's not God's heart towards it at all. He doesn't want us to feel like we're losing. If anything, surrendering to God actually means we are gaining more than we bargained for. It's a victory in itself.

Mark 8:36 AMP
For what does it benefit a man to gain the whole world [with all its pleasures], and forfeit his soul?

I've learnt and I am still learning that surrendering is an everyday decision; one we make in all aspects of life. When we wake up, we can choose to surrender our thoughts to God. When we go about our day, we are always making choices with what we do and how we feel about situations, people, life etc.

Luke 9:23 AMP
And He was saying to them all, "If anyone wishes to follow Me [as My disciple], he must deny himself [set aside selfish interests], and take up his cross daily [expressing a willingness to endure whatever may come] and follow Me [believing in Me, conforming to My example in living and, if need be, suffering or perhaps dying because of faith in Me].

Surrender is about being aware of these choices and making a conscious decision to become dependent on God. It stems from a heart posture of bowing ourselves before The King, becoming obedient, taking on humility and allowing Him to take control.

This doesn't mean we drop life and become robots. In fact, the more time we spend in building our relationship with Jesus, the more we willingly yield to His ways. If you're anything like me, feeling like you need to be in control and giving that up can be a big challenge. This is something I had to learn as I grew older in my faith. Although God had proven Himself to be true and faithful time and time again, my human nature would get the better of me and I would fall into old habits of control. It was all I knew growing up. As humans, we are prone to stuff up, but how wonderful it is to know that even when we do, God is there to pick us up each time. It doesn't give us an excuse to keep falling back into the patterns of the world, but it does remind us that His grace is sufficient and desiring to reflect the very heart of Christ on a daily basis is a part of our surrender.

Surrendering goes hand in hand with humility. As humans, it can be so easy to have our pride stand in the way, to take control and live life selfishly, but then if things aren't going as planned, we tend to blame God and expect a quick fix. We can't know every single detail of God's plan for our lives instantly, however, as we trust in God, He'll direct us step by step along the way. God's plans for our lives may not always go the way we intend it to go and it may not always be an easy path to take. Whatever it may look like, let me assure you that it is one worth journeying on, where He is able to provide a peace that surpasses all understanding, even when you can be experiencing complete turmoil.

When I seemed to have hit one of the lowest points in my life, surrender felt like my only option, when it should have been my first. When I felt like I had been exhausted from being in control of my life all the time and had completely worn myself out, it's like Jesus became the only light I saw, when really He had been there all along. It was me who had chosen to be in the darkness. Ann Voskamp words it so well in her book 'The Broken Way':

'How many woods, how many wildernesses have I found myself in? Had I known: God takes us into wildernesses not to abandon us—but to be alone with us? Wildernesses are not where God takes us to hurt us—but where He speaks to our hearts.'[1]

This is something I truly understood when I chose to look at it from the perspective of God's heart and not to my own selfish thinking. In hardships, it can be so easy to turn into a hermit crab, hide in our shells and ignore the rest of the world because let's be honest, sometimes it feels nice to wallow in our own self pity. But those are the times when God desires our time, affection and our attention the most. The vulnerable moments aren't there to con-

---

1   Ann Voskamp, 'The Broken Way', *William K. Jensen Literary Agency*, p. 219

demn or shame us, but for God to speak directly to our hearts and to be assured of His love and grace. Looking back now, it surprises me to think about how I ever lived my life without recognising His presence surrounding me daily. If anything, it's His very presence, to this day, that provides supernatural peace and joy in whatever challenge comes my way. He can do the same for you.

THREE

Defender

Time always goes by quicker than we realise. One moment I'm a 17 year-old girl trying to get my life together and the next I'm a 29 year old woman still being mistaken for an 18 year old… All credit to my Filipino genes. Sometimes I sit and ponder on how I ever survived my past without full reliance on Him. The Bible says it best: time is fleeting, it is but a vapour.

James 4:14 AMP
Yet you do not know [the least thing] about what may happen in your life tomorrow. [What is secure in your life?] You are merely a vapor

[like a puff of smoke or a wisp of steam from a cooking pot] that is visible for a little while and then vanishes [into thin air]."

As each day passes, I'm learning to be more intentional with the choices I make in life. This may seem like a very simple concept, but by intentionally choosing to remember the sacrifice Jesus made for us on a daily basis, while recognising that it's our Father who gives us grace from messy situations in our past, we can humbly come to a place where we surrender our hearts all the more.

Psalm 77:11 AMP
"I will [solemnly] remember the deeds of the Lord; Yes, I will [wholeheartedly] remember Your wonders of old.

As I mentioned in previous chapters, I had to learn everything the difficult way, but God knew that this was the best way for me to get it into my system. For you it may be different, or it may even be similar. However it comes about, embrace the process, allow Jesus to build a home in you and watch your life flourish.

Below is a large chunk of my personal journal that I had written after facing one of my toughest hurdles in life. I thought it was hard enough having to encounter the break up as a teenager going into early womanhood, but it was that experience that was able to equip me for my way later on in life. This recount delves into the deeper parts of my story; a testimony showing the heartache I endeavoured in my break up (at the time) with my husband Alexi, in order to come out the other side being strengthened by God alone. By choosing to live in remembrance of who He is, I was reminded of His overwhelming goodness and grace; a place of safety and an avenue for honest surrender to take place in my heart.

Journal Entry - 24/4/19

I believe it was God who allowed this break up between Alexi and I to take place. I believe it was during this time that God wanted to remind me of His limitless love and unending grace, regardless of my forgetful nature. Despite my recklessness and lack of surrender, He had an endless amount of grace for me, but while He was pouring it out, He wanted me to remember how much He truly loved me and I needed to re-learn how to reciprocate that love before moving forward. God needed to strip away a long-term relationship to deliver me from internal root issues that I had tried so hard to forget about or ignore and to remind me of complete surrender in Him alone. I never really acknowledged it, but deep down I knew I had rejection issues through my upbringing and my parents divorcing. Because of my broken family past, I had a distorted view of love and would find ways to fill that void. Before dating Alexi, I was in a physically and emotionally abusive relationship for four years - I had lost my virginity at seventeen and at the time felt like I needed to stick around to sustain that happiness. I battled within myself and stuck around in fear of not being able to find anything better. When God rescued me from that dark place, I again forgot about His goodness and how He pulled me out of destruction, causing me to fall back into a cycle of my old mentality, lifestyle and behavioural habits. Before Alexi, I would subtly make guys want me, then withdraw when we would get too close. I wouldn't necessarily be in relationships with these guys or even want a serious relationship with them; I simply enjoyed the attention. If an attractive guy gave me the attention I was longing for, I would reciprocate that and make them feel valued and wanted. It was all an emotional response to feel validated and desired. At the time I didn't see what was wrong with it because it all seemed like innocent fun, but looking back now, I realise that I had entertained something that would have further consequences down the track.

Years went by and throughout the stages of Alexi pursuing me, I genuinely started to like him a lot and actually considered being in a long term relationship with him—something that I had stopped myself from thinking about or going forward with since the bad experience of my failed seventeen year-old relationship. I didn't want to fall back into old patterns so I told myself that it wouldn't be the same, especially because Alexi hadn't ever had a girlfriend and seemed so pure in every way. We dated for four amazing years and later, after the four-year mark, that's when our world flipped upside down. It was 2018 where Alexi and I went through some difficult relationship issues. We had both contributed in our own ways towards the lead up of our break up, however the final straw was when I had lost Alexi's trust. That year he broke up with me and at that moment, we were a complete wreck. It was the most I had ever seen him cry in the period of us dating. In hindsight I'm so grateful that his obedience to God's voice overrode the desire to want to stay. His obedience allowed the healing to take place within the both of us. Although Alexi didn't want to break up, he knew it was what we needed to do. Deep down I knew it was probably better for us too, but I just wasn't ready to let go. I didn't want to surrender him to God. I couldn't. What would life look like without him? Who was I going to talk to about my day and my problems? I could see my entire life with this man and in one moment it was stripped from me. I started to realise that over the years I had made an idol of Alexi and prioritised him over the relationship with my Heavenly Father. It became clearer to me that I longed for him more than I did communion with God.

After the break up, I remember doing everything I could naturally to try and change his mind. I dressed nicely, I told him how much he still meant to me, I did everything humanly possible to try to work things out, but none of it worked. Alexi was firm on his decision, without giving any hope that we would ever get back together. I still remember the conversation we had with him telling me not to wait for him, that God would have to bring complete peace about us if we were ever to happen and that was the last of our conversation. I remember feeling angry, completely distraught and physically sick to my stomach. My friends and family would get worried about me because I was losing a lot of weight in such a short amount of time. I just couldn't eat properly or even talk without bursting into tears. Every thought of Alexi would make me cry, or I would feel sick and lose my appetite. This break up ate away at me. I was so full of rage and had to battle through unforgiveness within myself. And to think it couldn't have gotten any worse, a few weeks after we had broken up, I was told by his mum that he had planned on proposing to me when I came back from my holiday overseas. This was a really trialing time for me when I had heard this. It put me through a lot of emotional heartache, with some days feeling like I couldn't cope at all.

Firstly, I caught up with Kelly (my pastor at the time and a close friend of mine) and she suggested that I write a letter to him, expressing how I felt and leaving it at that. I dropped it off to his house at a time I knew he wouldn't be home and from then he never gave me any signs of whether he had read it or not. I just had to assume he had. Throughout the couple of months (which felt like a lifetime) of us being broken up, that was just it—God was teaching me to be okay with the mystery and the unknown; to be content with not having control and being able to trust Him, despite the storm surrounding me. He was teaching me the posture of complete worship and surrender, restructuring how I viewed love and giving me the opportunity to fall back in love with His presence. As much as I hated not knowing how Alexi was feeling on his end, God was reminding me that the ease and peace shouldn't have to come from what Alexi was feeling, but to come from everything God had to offer. I had to slowly learn throughout the next couple of months that I had to be okay with whatever the outcome was. I had to be okay with whether Alexi ended up with me or not because ultimately it wasn't even about getting back with him, but it was about putting God first, trusting in Him for the unknown areas in my future and falling in love with His presence all over again. God also needed to deal with issues in my heart that would block me from becoming a Godly wife and leader. I wrote out a list of things that I needed specific prayer on and decided to pray over it every night.

I caught up with Aunty Nazra (a woman of unapologetic faith, who I grew up with as a second mum) and Kelly a lot as the elder women in my life to keep accountable to about everything. Aunty Nazra mentioned a man was coming down to Adelaide who, through the power of The Holy Spirit, delivered people from all sorts of struggles, such as addiction, spiritual bondage, fears... the list goes on and so I went to see him. Although he prayed over me and I didn't feel anything instantly, I knew that God saw my hunger of genuinely wanting to be healed from past hurts.

It really was a difficult journey to go through, having to wake up everyday, verbally speaking out and declaring God's goodness, despite feeling like absolute trash in the natural. Throughout the time I spent away from Alexi, God was able to speak to and through me in so many beautiful ways. I read His word everyday and so many books; books that spoke directly to my situation and pretty much hit the core of what I was feeling. There were many scriptures and book references that would relate to what I was going through. It was as if God was reassuring me that Alexi and I would eventually work things out, but there was always a vagueness to this promise. Convinced it was just my mind playing tricks on me, I continued to shrug off these ideas and since I didn't want to be obsessed or linger over the promise itself, I chose to solely concentrate on the rebuilding of my relationship with God. I had to surrender everything back to Him and not keep anything for myself. Sentimental things are a big deal to me and so to show God that I was serious about surrendering the relationship without putting my hope IN IT, immediately after prayer time with God, I deleted all Alexi's pictures off my Instagram (bear in mind, this was a huge deal for me, as I didn't just archive them, but I completely deleted them). I also took everything that reminded me of him that I owned of his and gave it to my good friend Alice for her to keep from me. Originally I had planned to give it back to Alexi or give it away as donations to an op shop, but Alice told me that she would keep it. I then deleted all his pictures from my phone, convinced that I would never see them again. I even untagged myself in photos on Facebook where he was in (talk about being dramatic... thanks Mum for the traits I picked up from you). Visually, I couldn't put myself in a position where he would be associated with me. When I was at church, I would try to avoid him as much as I could, when at the start, I would still long to be seen by him or to see him. I just found that in order to take this sacrifice seriously, I needed to act upon it with wisdom and so I decided to lay all that I had of Alexi on the altar, as heartbreaking as it all was at the time.

It was a rebuilding and renewal of my love and relationship in God: putting Him first, despite the mystery and the heartache. Amidst the self blaming and struggling to forgive myself, God was still showing me His grace. He was reassuring me that He was my redeemer. I didn't want to put all of my hope in getting back with Alexi, but to keep my focus on God. I chose not to hold onto the thought of winning Alexi back, instead pressing further into God's presence. As the days went by, the books I would read and verses were always so encouraging, despite feeling down at times and God continuously reminded me that He was with me. I found myself falling more and more in love with

God and I would get excited to go home, just to spend more time with Him. I had also made a decision not to listen to secular love songs so that I wouldn't become controlled by emotional thoughts, but instead chose to listen to worship songs about God and His nature, so I could draw closer to Him. It was in those moments with God where I made a commitment to stay single for a year, until He told me otherwise.

The day Alexi and I actually decided to work things out was months later. It was on a Sunday morning and I wasn't expecting it all; I was just content that God was guiding me through the toughness of the season. By that point I felt so immersed in God and things were looking up. I remember seeing Alexi at our City church campus, which he wasn't supposed to be at, because he was originally rostered on for our Paradise church campus, but apparently he had been swapped to do photography for the baptisms at City. Although we noticed one another, we didn't really say hi to each other and just carried on with our duties. Ps Tony was preaching a word about being in a storm and still choosing to move forward. He then proceeded to say that he felt there were some people or someone in the room who was wondering whether to go forward with a decision and that God was saying "Yes", to believe that He could still bring restoration in the midst of the storm.

I remember a thought coming in mind, thinking that this word could be relevant to our situation, but brushing it off seconds after.

HONEST SURRENDER

About a minute later, I received a message from Alexi asking if I was free after church to catch-up (bear in mind, Alexi and I hadn't spoken since the awkward closure, so getting a message from him, you could imagine made me a little excited and confused at the same time). After church, we ended up going to our favourite restaurant (when we used to date) and just chatted like normal. We then went out for dessert afterwards and that's when we opened up a little more. Alexi was telling me how all week he was struggling to find peace and that The Holy Spirit had said to him that he would have peace about his answer at the end of the week (the Sunday), that he would know what to do from there. Although Alexi had signs throughout that week, he mentioned that it was Ps Tony's word which brought about the peace and direction from God to bring restoration into our relationship again.

This time around, Alexi and I decided to do things the right way and to again put God above everything. The day after we officially got back together, I was prompted to read Philemon. I thought this was quite unusual because I hadn't looked into this book a whole lot, but when I did, the first thing I read was highlighted to me and it made me incredibly emotional. The verse said:

Philemon 1:15
"Perhaps the reason he was separated from you for a little while was that you might have him back forever."

At first, my understanding on this was, "Wow, thank you God that Alexi and I were separated and we both went through a season of refining, so he and I could work things out forever", but now I realise that Alexi was separated from me so that I could be refined in God and find love in the relationship with God forever. It had always been about God from the beginning.

Two days after Alexi had asked me out to lunch to tell me that he wanted to pursue a future with me and work things out (a day after The Holy Spirit had prompted me to read Philemon 1:15), these words were highlighted to me from Francine Rivers' book, 'A Lineage of Grace':

"Her spirit rejoiced in Jesus, her Saviour. All her life, she had struggled to find answers, to rise above her circumstances, to obey God and wait——not always patiently——for his plan to unfold, and now she was filled with awe at what God had done. She had mourned and was comforted with the promise of life eternal with him. She had hungered and thirsted for justice, and now beheld the one who would judge. Mary fell to her knees before Jesus and bowed her head to the ground. "My Lord," she said in complete surrender. "My Lord and God."[2]

---

2   Francine Rivers, 'A Lineage of Grace', *Tyndale House Publishers Inc.*, p. 524

HONEST SURRENDER

Reading this section of the book was extremely emotional for me. It was as if God was confirming His hand over our relationship and reminding me of the promise He had fulfilled through our obedience and surrender.

Sidenote: the pictures I had completely deleted off my phone miraculously turned back up on my storage and I was able to retrieve every single photo that had been previously deleted. Even though this was a small part of the bigger picture, I'm so glad that God took an interest in even the small things I care about.

All this to say, I look back and I'm overwhelmed by God's goodness. I'm humbled by this whole experience and will always know my God as my loving and gracious Father, who will stop at nothing to provide all that He has for His children. I'm so undeserving and yet He still blessed me with more than I could have asked for. I'm now engaged to Alexi and I'm always in remembrance of the fact that God is TRUE to His promises. Surrender isn't about expecting or receiving anything as a prize back from God. Surrender is more than that. Simply knowing that He loves me back, with an unconditional love, will always be enough. Because of this, my response is surrender - no hidden agendas, just complete and absolute surrender, because HE is enough. He is sufficient in all things and nothing or no one can convince me otherwise.

As I faced my battles, it was God who was fighting for me and defending me from what the enemy meant for harm. For all of us, there is always an everyday battle to face: health and financial battles, relationship battles, battles in the mind... The list could go on and on. In whatever we encounter, it's always a daily choice to be in remembrance of how faithful God is and to recognise that He is our defender through it all. One of the verses that I really clung onto during my season of heartache was Psalms 144:1-2 AMP:

"Blessed be the Lord, my Rock and my great strength, who trains my hands for war and my fingers for battle; my [steadfast] lovingkindness and my fortress, my high tower and my rescuer, my shield and He in whom I take refuge, who subdues my people under me."

King David, who was one of the principal contributors to the book of Psalms, shows us that despite what he was facing, he recognised that God was his defender and the reason for his victories. It was God who constantly protected him, but not only that, it was also the same God who taught him *how to* fight. In the same way for our lives, we aren't left to fend for ourselves, but as we go through trials in life, we are given the opportunity to either rely on ourselves or to turn to God as our rock. In Wendy Pope's book

'Wait And See', she shows us the power in waiting, as well as what our focus during the wait should be on. 'It is during these times that we have to fight to maintain our focus on the Person of our faith rather than the object of our wait,'[3] she says.

For my own life, I was able to recognise God as my defender, defending me against the enemy and his plans to make me fearful for the future, filling my mind with constant worry and lingering on unforgiveness in myself. I had to learn to lean into God and let go of insecurities, control, fear and many other thoughts, which were holding me back. It was a daily choice to put my trust in God and to actively remember the good things He had done for me. If I had seen victories in my life before, what would stop God from doing them again? Rather than waiting for the next big promise to come along, I was focusing on *who* God was. It was Him who was equipping me to fight through hardships in the future, but not only that, He was preparing me to empower those who also find themselves in a similar boat. I know He would want me to remind them that He is our defender, our rock, our protector, and as long as we are making those daily decisions to trust Him and surrender everything as a whole, we will see such a change from where we started to wherever God takes us in our future.

---

3 Wendy Pope, 'Wait And See', *David C Cook*, p. 37

FOUR

Touch Of Heaven

Going through the break up was one of the most painful hurdles I had to face. Knowing that Alexi and I were prominent leaders in our church, I remember feeling ashamed, like a complete failure and that's where the enemy thought he had won me over. I also felt the pressure of having to keep my life together and had somehow fallen back into the mindset of being self-reliant. Through Paul David Tripp's words, we are able to recognise how crucial it is to be aware of how we handle suffering through what it exposes:

'Suffering has the power to expose our self-reliance. Suffering has the power to expose our self-righteousness. Suffering has the power to lay waste to our idols.'[4]

Although it was hard to go through the suffering, as well as the process of healing, it was exactly what I needed in order to experience true freedom. I made the choice to repent and to surrender it all back to God again and again. I had to actively seek out personal freedom classes and encounter deliverance for past root issues, through prayer. It took a lot of time and dedication, but I was willing to give that all up to see complete liberation take place within me. To experience His peace, joy and freedom, it always requires some kind of sacrifice and for me, that required giving up my control, which depended highly on self-reliance.

When we choose to shift our eyes off of ourselves and look at it from God's perspective, we realise that these sacrifices are ones worth taking. My mum says it well and over the years has reminded me that often: surrendering is a form of victory. And she's absolutely right. By surrendering, now I'm able to stand in confidence and know that I had to go through inconvenience, discomfort and pain to experience true peace, patience and grace. I had fought too hard, cried too many tears, prayed relentlessly and

---

4   Paul David Tripp, 'Suffering', *Crossway*, p. 181-182

stayed up too many nights for the enemy to ever come and steal my joy again.

Whenever family and close friends ask if I would go through the pain again, I know my place in God enough to respond and say yes. I honestly would. I mean, it would be difficult experiencing the emotional turmoil of it all, but if I knew it would produce a new kind of me, one who chooses Christ over myself, then yes, I would do it all over again. Maybe you have found yourself dealing with a similar journey as myself, or maybe you're trudging through and still trying to find yourself amidst all the messiness. The enemy wants us to believe that we can't escape what we're dealing with, but Jesus brings complete freedom.

Galatians 5:1 AMP
It was for this freedom that Christ set us free [completely liberating us]; therefore keep standing firm and do not be subject again to a yoke of slavery [which you once removed].

The enemy warps our minds to believe that the sins we have entangled ourselves in are inescapable and if we have fallen prey to his manipulation and made mistakes, I'm here to tell you that God's grace is more than enough and the freedom He offers is for everyone. I had to learn to forgive myself, but I didn't do it all alone. I first had to surrender what I had, then choose to surrender daily. It was only then that God was able to work the healing process within me. Maybe you're in a place of the in between. As you're reading this, you may even be feeling the tug of The Holy Spirit telling you to let go of something or someone and in that prompting, you're trying to muster up the strength to surrender it to Him. Commune with Him, pray, meditate on His Word and ask Him to give you His supernatural strength when you're feeling weak.

2 Corinthians 12:9 AMP
But He has said to me, "My grace is sufficient for you [My lovingkindness and My mercy are more than enough—always available—regardless of the situation]; for [My] power is being perfected [and is completed and shows itself most effectively] in [your] weakness. Therefore, I will all the more gladly boast in my weaknesses, so that the power of Christ [may completely enfold me and] may dwell in me."

The peace and liberation that comes from this can only truly be experienced when we choose to give it to Him. Jesus is knocking at the doors of our heart and it's up to us as to whether we let Him in or not.

Revelation 3:20 AMP
Behold, I stand at the door [of the church] and continually knock. If anyone hears My voice and opens the door, I will come in and eat with him (restore him), and he with Me."

It's in the daily choice to remember what Jesus has done for us on the cross and how He saved us from our own past that helps to open our eyes towards surrender. No longer do we have to live feeling like we need to be in complete control 24/7—control can be so overrated and exhausting anyway. Let's take Abraham for instance. His story in the Bible is one that demonstrates such a remarkable act of surrender. We see this in Genesis 22:1-19, where he is tested to sacrifice his son. Now when we read this, it almost seems cruel that God would even ask of him such a thing. If I were Abraham, I probably would've slowed down the conversation and asked the first obvious question... WHY THOUGH... LIKE REALLY GOD, IS THIS NECESSARY?! But as the story unravels, Abraham didn't even question God or His intentions; he just followed through and proceeded to obey God's command. We even see in verses 3-5 that Abraham wakes up early (talk about eager obedience) and decides to worship God before sacrificing Isaac.

Genesis 22:3-5 AMP

So Abraham got up early in the morning, saddled his donkey, and took two of his young men with him and his son Isaac; and he split the wood for the burnt offering, and then he got up and went to the place of which God had told him. On the third day [of travel] Abraham looked up and saw the place in the distance. Abraham said to his servants, "Settle down and stay here with the donkey; the young man and I will go over there and worship [God], and we will come back to you."

It seems to me that Abraham had a huge amount of confidence and trust in God, unflinching to the request asked of him. Over the timeline of Abraham's life, there are two comparisons that stick out to me about his willingness to surrender.

1) In verse 2 of Genesis 22, God reminds Abraham that Isaac is his only son and even emphasizes on the fact that he loves him.

Genesis 22:2 AMP

God said, "Take now your son, your only son [of promise], whom you love, Isaac, and go to the region of Moriah, and offer him there as a burnt offering on one of the mountains of which I shall tell you."

Why didn't God simply say, "Take Isaac and sacrifice him on this mountain"? Why did God have to emphasize on Isaac being his only son? Why did God have to remind Abraham of the great love he had for Isaac? Surely God could have kept things short, sharp and shiny. I believe the reason God was being particular with what He needed to say was because He was giving Abraham the opportunity to assess his priorities to see where his trust, obedience and surrender truly lay. Was it in the protection of his son, or was it in God, the God who had given Isaac to Abraham in the first place? Although Abraham would have been fully aware of the fact that Isaac was his son and that he dearly loved him, knowing that God was aware of how much Isaac meant to him would have really put Abraham in a position of honest surrender.

Sometimes we choose to surrender things that don't necessarily make us budge and avoid the things that God is actually asking of us. The moment God becomes more specific in asking us to surrender things closer to our heart, we become protective and back away. For me it was, "Take Alexi, the one you've been dating for four years and love deeply. Sacrifice him to me and I will give you direction. Take your control, the way of security that you have been clinging to for so long. Surrender it to me and I will show you how." God doesn't want us to compromise surrender or find ways to bargain with surrender, He is simply looking for our honest surrender; one that doesn't question, but willingly submits to His ways. When you look at your life, what are the specific things

God is waiting on you to surrender? It could be a job, a position, material things, a relationship or an attitude. Whatever it may be, Abraham exemplifies a powerful act of obedience in surrendering; one that we can take into account and really consider for our response to God in our own lives.

2) In the previous chapters of Abraham's life, we read in Genesis 17 that he was promised a son by God.

Genesis 17:19 AMP
"But God said, "No, Sarah your wife shall bear you a son indeed, and you shall name him Isaac (laughter); and I will establish My covenant with him for an everlasting covenant and with his descendants after him."

As well as being promised a son, Abraham is also given the promise from God that he would have descendants as numerous as the stars in the sky.

Genesis 26:4 AMP
"I will make your descendants multiply as the stars of the heavens, and will give to your descendants all these lands; and by your descendants shall all the nations of the earth be blessed."

He was promised an overwhelming amount of blessing. After Abraham had been told these promises, we see Sarai convince Abraham to sleep with his maid, Hagar, as she was unable to bear children.

Genesis 16:1-2 AMP

"Now Sarai, Abram's wife, had not borne him any children, and she had an Egyptian maid whose name was Hagar. So Sarai said to Abram, "See here, the Lord has prevented me from bearing children. I am asking you to go into [the bed of] my maid [so that she may bear you a child]; perhaps I will obtain children by her." And Abram listened to Sarai and did as she said."

Here we are shown the difference between Abraham's trust and response when it came to God's promise in his earlier days in comparison to his latter years, when he was asked to sacrifice Isaac. In this case, Abraham chose to compromise his surrender of trust by giving in to the ideas of his wife. This was not what God had originally intended. Over time, when Abraham was asked to sacrifice Isaac, we see a change in the way he chooses to respond to God and his willingness to surrender. This no longer being compromised. He was able to learn from his past mistakes and realised that God didn't need help for his promises to be fulfilled. All he needed to offer to God was his trust, obedience and honest surrender. I know for my own life, I've seen time and time again how faithful God has been, yet there have been moments where I've offered to speed up the process by choosing to do things my own way. God is fully capable of bringing about the promise in His perfect timing. He certainly doesn't need our help to do so. In His Word, He promises blessings for all of our lives, but how will we choose to respond to Him? Let's be people who never forget the goodness and faithfulness God has shown us, but instead cling tight to Him, despite how difficult our situation may seem at the time.

There's one person who demonstrates the ultimate surrender, one who is unmatched. Jesus paid the price willingly so that we could live in freedom.

Luke 22:42 AMP
"Father, if You are willing, remove this cup [of divine wrath] from Me; yet not My will, but [always] Yours be done."

Jesus came down from heaven to experience everything we experience as humans — temptation, hurt, fear, judgment. He went through it all. He surrendered His position of royalty and even His life because of how much He loves us. This supreme sacrifice ultimately saved us from living in eternal condemnation. If it weren't for Him, our sins would not have been atoned for and our access to Heaven would have been denied. Then there is the incredible example of our Father's heart, who sent His only son, Jesus, to sacrifice His life to save us from our sins. The Father exemplified surrender in such a way that He had to physically turn away when His son was dying on the cross. This would have been a difficult task to endure: for God to have watched His only son die for all of mankind, and yet there was no sign of pride in either of them to stop what was happening (even though they had the absolute power and authority to do so).

Looking at the lives of Jesus and God The Father surrendering themselves for us teaches that our choices of surrender not only affect our life, but also the lives around us. When we make a decision to lay aside pride and choose humility, we're choosing to live as Jesus did: pouring out God's love on strangers, friends, colleagues, family and people around us. When I was consumed with my own life and self desires, I forgot about others and only really catered to myself. The moment God's grace was truly experienced for my own life was the moment I was able to really consider others and recognise that there was so much more than just attending to my own needs. Surrendering myself to the ways of God changed my life for the better. My heart and attitude towards people, as well as my direction and my passion to serve others, became more diligent and selfless. As long as we're on this earth, we're continuously being given a daily choice of surrender. What will that look like for you today?

FIVE

Father's Love

I remember when I was a young kid. After lunchtime, we would go inside and play sleeping logs. For those of you who don't know the game, the aim of it is to spread out across the classroom while lying down and having to stay as still as a log. Almost every time, kids end up falling asleep and eventually get woken up when it's home time. I'm pretty sure the only reason we played that game was so that the teachers could get a break from all the crazy kids running around and not having to deal with the one little hungry Filipina kid (aka me), always asking when they could eat next... Honestly I don't know why I was so hungry all the time. This is still relevant to my life now. I'm just always hungry. I remember resting my eyes and using that time to try to figure out which kid I would talk to about Jesus the next day. I would even have a small conversation with Jesus in my head asking Him to show me, then I would go into a deep sleep, until my teacher would wake me up and tell me it's home time. Most days, I expected a face to pop up and the next day, I would make it my aim to mention Jesus to the classmate that I felt He had shown me. Even if a face didn't happen to come to mind, I would share it to whoever was close by. Looking back, I'm blown away by my faith, my trust in God and my level of surrender as a child. I had no worries in the world and just desired for other kids to know who He was. That was my world – Jesus. Somehow, along my maturing years, my mind became so caught up in other issues like school, self-image, boys and friends, but from this memory, there are a few simple things we can learn from little version me when it comes to surrender:

1. Trusting Jesus.
2. Being expectant.
3. Resting in Him.

Trusting Jesus

In His Word, Jesus talks about humbling ourselves to have childlike faith.

Matthew 18:24 AMP
He called a little child and set him before them, and said, "I assure you and most solemnly say to you, unless you repent [that is, change your inner self—your old way of thinking, live changed lives] and become like children [trusting, humble, and forgiving], you will never enter the kingdom of heaven. Therefore, whoever humbles himself like this child is greatest in the kingdom of heaven."

Just like I had easily put my trust in Jesus, having faith that He would show me which classmate to share the good news to, He too desires us to confidently look to Him as our source. As we grow older, we're corrupted by the ways of this world and as that corruption enters our mind, sometimes our response towards trusting Jesus can alter. When people I really cared about betrayed me and let me down, it affected the trust levels I had with others. When I had betrayed people who meant the most to me and let myself down, it made me reconsider trust levels even more. It made me think that if I couldn't even trust myself, knowing I was in control of my own actions, what hope do I have for other people and their intentions? It's these kinds of experiences that can distort our levels of trust with Him too. But Jesus isn't flawed like people are and that's what we fail to remember. Sometimes it can be hard to relate to Him as one of us, but we forget that He came to earth, experienced all the hurt, rejection and pain we felt as humans and even in His humanity, He *still* managed to be sinless. If He was able to conquer all of that as a mere human, imagine how much greater He is in all of His Holiness. Imagine how much more we're able to trust that He won't let us down with whatever we present to Him with the things we hold so dear to our hearts.

There is nothing that surprises Him. Nothing too large or too small that He can't heal, change and provide for. I've been in conversations with people who have said things like, "I've done too many bad things for even Jesus to forgive me. That's not for me, I'm too stuffed up. God wouldn't want any part of me." Sometimes we're the harshest on ourselves, when God is standing right by our side, desiring our attention. God knew us before we were even formed in our mother's womb.

Jeremiah 1:5 AMP
Before I formed you in the womb I knew you [and approved of you as My chosen instrument], and before you were born I consecrated you [to Myself as My own]; I have appointed you as a prophet to the nations.

What we've done doesn't change how much He loves us; it doesn't alter His desire to be near us and it doesn't take away His need to see us through. The cost of Jesus' life was so that we could be found completely in Him. Trusting can be difficult and nobody expects anyone to jump straight in, but it does require taking a step of faith, making a daily decision to open up our hearts in allowing Him to be a part of every aspect in our lives – whether that be in our best moments or in our weaker times.

Being Expectant

Being expectant asks questions like: "God, how will you show yourself today? How do you want to use me?" It requires preparation, patience, faith and complete trust in God.

Psalm 5:3 AMP
In the morning, O Lord, You will hear my voice; In the morning I will prepare [a prayer and a sacrifice] for You and watch and wait [for You to speak to my heart].

When I was younger and would ask Jesus which classmate He wanted me to share with them about His love, almost every time, I *expected* Him to show me a face. There were days when I wouldn't be shown a face at all, but as a child, that never discouraged me, neither did it affect my expectations to hope to see one the next day. I just didn't let it faze me and simply trusted Him. I didn't question why or seek any explanation as to why He hadn't shown me a face that day because I just knew in my heart that He was Jesus and being Jesus, that simply meant His reasons were valid and that He was trustworthy and good. Sometimes I look back on my younger self and I'm inspired by the way I viewed things. Nowadays, I need to constantly remind myself of His goodness and actively choose to be expectant.

As humans, of course it can be challenging, especially when we're completely open to seeing something happen and then nothing does. When that happens, I've learned (and am still learning) to see where my intentions lie. Am I upset that it didn't happen because it didn't go my way? Am I embarrassed that it didn't go the way I wanted it to because I put myself out there? When we re-evaluate the reasons behind the expectations of our heart, sometimes we can be taken aback by what God reveals to us. Over the last few years, God has shown me that being expectant is about believing in what He can do and eagerly waiting on Him, and even if those things don't happen at the time we expect, trusting that He is good regardless. 'Never be afraid to trust an unknown future to a known God.'[5]

---

5   Wendy Pope, 'Wait And See', *David C Cook*, p. 106

Resting in Him

I love my sleep and I love my naps. My body will naturally wake up early, but I'm the type of person who can easily go back to sleep, regardless if someone's talking or if the sun is beaming across my face. Now, when we think of rest, it can easily be associated with sleeping, but there is actually quite a difference. In an article that shows the comparisons between the two, it explains:

'Resting is being calm, but attentive to your surroundings. Sleep tunes out your environment and perception of your surroundings. During sleep, your brain goes through stages to tune out your environment and REM begins. This does not happen during resting.'[6]

Resting in Him doesn't mean shutting off everything and everyone else around us (like sleeping does), but it does mean giving ourselves time to just be still in His presence and experiencing the peace He offers, yet still being attentive with the work of God in our lives. Resting *in* Him allows our source of strength to be drawn *from* Him, so that we aren't wearing ourselves out.

---

6   [Online] Available at: https://thatsleepguy.com/difference-between-resting-and-sleeping/ [Accessed 28th November, 2019]

HONEST SURRENDER

Matthew 11:29 AMP
Take My yoke upon you and learn from Me [following Me as My disciple], for I am gentle and humble in heart, and you will find rest (renewal, blessed quiet) for your souls.

Sometimes we can be easily distracted by the busyness of life itself, but by finding rest in God, we're able to take a breather, direct our attention back to Him and embrace those beautiful moments of peace and refreshment to our spirit.

Have you ever been in a position where there's one last chicken sitting on a plate, there's only two of you at the table and you know in that moment you've both just entered The Hunger Games - aka the first person to grab the chicken loses (or wins, depending on what perspective you're looking at it from). Now imagine this scenario taking place: Although your body and appetite is telling you to grab the chicken and eat it to satisfy your own desires, your heart is cautioning you to consider the other person who is also in the same predicament as you. It would be easy to eat the chicken, but then you would be robbing the other person of satisfying their appetite, so instead of taking it for yourself, you decide to leave it for your friend. Although it has left you hungry at that moment, you walk away feeling good that you were able to give it to them instead.

A couple of weeks later, you end up catching up with them and because they were so impressed with you surrendering the last piece of chicken, they decide to buy you a lifetime supply of chicken (the fact that I even used food as an analogy to get my point across is beyond me... This is what I mean: I'm always thinking about food.) So I know this is a highly unlikely situation, but isn't this what surrendering to God can sometimes feel like? It can be so easy to satisfy our fleshly desires. Giving in to what we want may feel good in that particular moment, but when we choose to sacrifice that to Him, it is nothing in comparison to the lifetime supply of peace, liberation and living out the promised blessings that God offers when we choose to surrender.

Journal Entry - 20/8/18

Right now I'm focusing on knowing who I am in God, finding my complete identity in Him again and not having to worry about what Alexi thinks of me as an overall. I'm learning to let go of Alexi's thoughts about me, because ultimately God is dealing with him on his end. I don't at all need to know the process going on with him. It doesn't mean I immediately try to switch off loving Alexi, but it does mean that I stop feeling the need to be in control of knowing everything and instead putting trust in God when the unknown arises. It means me not looking into things and not making assumptions, as well as avoiding trying to make sense of everything. God will allow everything to turn out the way He intends and during this process, I need to make room for it, be okay with not knowing, simply trust Him and find peace in that.

I had written a journal entry during my break up period about finding myself in Christ again because along the way I had distracted myself and placed my identity in other things. When we put our identity in anything but Christ, we are manipulated to believe that being in control of our own lives causes a successful and freeing life, but by doing this, we are actually limiting ourselves. In my case, I had prioritised my identity in Alexi and the relationship. To be honest, I was completely oblivious to the fact that I had done this, until Alexi and I broke up. It's not like I had intentionally put him above Jesus, but I wasn't careful with my everyday choice to surrender. I genuinely loved Jesus and thought my relationship with Him was going fine, but it was in the complacent behaviour where I had become too comfortable. Although Jesus was tugging at my heart, I seemed to be more invested in putting my identity in the relationship with Alexi, rather than in Christ. A re-prioritising needed to take place and unfortunately at the time, it was at the cost of losing Alexi. When I was aware of this, I went on a journey of finding my identity in Jesus again and being reminded through scriptures like Ephesians 2:10, that I was created *in* Christ and this made me come to appreciate all that He had saved me from.

Ephesians 2:10 AMP
(For we are His workmanship [His own master work, a work of art], created in Christ Jesus [reborn from above—spiritually transformed, renewed, ready to be used] for good works, which God prepared [for us] beforehand [taking paths which He set], so that we would walk in them [living the good life which He prearranged and made ready for us]).

When I think about my identity in Christ, I'm reminded of another situation where God really highlighted Himself and caused a greater outcome towards believing that Truth. Throughout mine and Alexi's engagement, everything seemed to be complete bliss. The biggest issue we fussed over was what kind of chairs we would use for the reception. Hardly an argument, if you ask me. During that time, I really thought marriage life would be nice and cruisy. God came and humbled me big time. Around three months out from getting married, that's when the opposition decided to make his move yet again. Amidst the commotion of COVID-19, a flu-like virus that had taken the world by storm and caused everyone to panic-buy endless amounts of toilet paper (due to self-isolation laws), Alexi and I were suffering our own relationship pain. Issues from Alexi's past resurfaced that had once affected me deeply and I was forced to deal with the hurt of rebuilding that trust with him. There was a two-week period where we fought over this matter and it felt like it consumed my mind.

At one stage we even foolishly considered whether we would go through with the marriage or not. Eventually we were able to think more clearly and realised that we had conquered these hurts before so why were we acting like we had been defeated? The enemy had caught us at a weak moment and decided to use that to his advantage, putting negative thoughts in my mind and attempting to make us forget about the authority we held inside of us. As frustrated as I was, God reminded me of who I was to Him and how precious I am.

Isaiah 43:4 ESV
"Because you are precious in my eyes, and honored, and I love you, I give men in return for you, peoples in exchange for your life."

I was given the strength to recognise that we are His precious children and our identity was found in Him being a Father who never leaves us nor forsakes us. I was again reminded that God was the core of this relationship and it gave me the authority to boldly call out the enemy for what he was: a liar, one who is only out to kill, steal and destroy. With God by our side, Alexi and I eventually fought our way through this together. We would have never been able to make it this far if it weren't for God Himself. He is sovereign and He is good, even when the enemy will try to catch us out at our most vulnerable times. When you find yourself in those moments and are completely taken off guard, remind yourself of who you belong to and who you are in God. This will always, without a doubt, give you the upper hand because He has already won the victory and He lives inside of you. Satan can try his hardest to prod us with insecurities, lies and accusations, but you can be certain that by belonging to God, it means you have already conquered them. The One who is living in you is far greater than anything that tries to come against you.

1 John 4:4 TPT
Little children, you can be certain that you belong to God and have conquered them, for the One who is living in you is far greater than the one who is in the world.

We are forgiven, free, an heir to His riches and inheritance, chosen, appointed and unconditionally loved. We don't need anyone or anything else to define us, because our identity is already found in Him; our source of strength and the one who brings us

HONEST SURRENDER

peace amidst the searching. Knowing that I once lived in my own control and complacency helps me gauge my levels of surrender and trust in Him on an everyday basis and this can be the same for you. Whenever we're feeling down or discouraged, instead of focusing on how we're feeling or what we're facing, we can choose to remember who we are in Christ and how God sees us.

Ephesians 1:4 NIV
For he chose us in Him before the creation of the world to be holy and blameless in his sight.

SIX

Even When It Hurts

Overcoming adversary can sometimes be intimidating, disheartening and very draining, but it doesn't have to be like this. In my personal freedom classes that I attended, we were reminded that we're living *from* victory — victory of Jesus dying on the cross and being raised to life again.

Revelation 1:18 AMP
and the Ever-living One [living in and beyond all time and space]. I died, but see, I am alive forevermore, and I have the keys of [absolute control and victory over] death and of Hades (the realm of the dead).

HONEST SURRENDER

The enemy could not hold Jesus down and has already been defeated, therefore we have the upper hand because ultimately we have God on our side. This may already seem like information we know, but it's essential to remind ourselves of this daily. I know for my own mind, I can be so forgetful in nature, or the busyness of life just comes and makes its way in. I'm constantly making a choice to remember how much Jesus has actually done for me, knowing that if it weren't for His sacrifice, I wouldn't even be here to begin with. A heart of genuine gratefulness will often lead to a place of humility because we're remembering where we came from and it was never ourselves who brought us to where we are right now. Sure, we may have made decisions that led to these moments, but ultimately it was The Father's heart who chose for His only son to be a willing sacrifice, as well as Jesus Himself taking on the responsibility of self-sacrifice, so that we could even step foot on earth. This can have a huge impact on the way we choose to live our everyday lives. Having a consistent attitude of thankfulness and humility can eliminate pride; pride being one of the main things that can separate us from knowing Him in more depth.

When we choose to consistently take a moment each day to just spend time with God and make it a priority to thank Him for every big or even small thing that He has done for us, I assure you that this act of surrender will build you up for long term gain.

Carrying a heart of gratitude recognises God's grace, pushes away pride and helps you look at life in a way that affects your everyday attitudes and decisions to be like Christ.

1 Thessalonians 5:18 AMP
In every situation [no matter what the circumstances] be thankful and continually give thanks to God; for this is the will of God for you in Christ Jesus.

People also tend to gravitate towards those who have a heart of gratitude, especially those who are having a hard time or are struggling in life, because it gives them hope that they too can find peace and joy in even the small appreciations of life. Gratitude gradually helps to produce a mindset that can also become others focused because when you truly recognise how good God has been in your own life, then you also desire the same for others. It can be so easy to go through life and forget to thank God for what He's done, but when we intentionally choose to put time aside and simply thank Him, surrendering goes from being something we read in the scriptures, to something we live and breathe everyday.

When Alexi and I broke up, I remember most of my prayers still involved thanking God for my life, for the process and for guiding me through. I would even thank Him for things that hadn't yet come because I believed that even when I was hurting, what

He had promised in His Word would eventually come to pass for my own life. There were days where it would take everything to muster up the strength to pray and be thankful, but every time I did, I never regretted it once. There was one particular moment I clearly remember during the break up where I chose gratitude and praise over the issue and it really brought light into my situation. I had just bought noodles from Wok In A Box for dinner, as I hadn't eaten all day, but even after one mouthful I felt physically sick. I couldn't even eat it (when usually I would demolish that meal in 0.5 seconds and then buy a second one). I knew that this break up had affected my health and that my friends and doctors were worried about me, but I just couldn't muster up the strength to eat. I was so frustrated at myself for rejecting the food and then at that point, negative thoughts started to fill my head.

Over that period of time I had lost so much weight and during each day I would either feel physically weak or lethargic all the time. I never really had issues when it came to eating food before, so this was all really new for me. I remember I just sat there in my car sobbing for a while and when I would catch a breath, I would sob even more. It was one of my harder days where I couldn't stop thinking about Alexi and so amidst all the messiness and ugly crying (my face turns into something else when I'm crying), I decided I needed to pray. All I kept repeating over and over again was,

"God, you're so good to me. I thank you for this life. You're so good to me, I thank you for everything". If you saw how ruined I looked and compared it to what I was saying, you probably would have been really confused, but the more I thanked God, the lighter I felt. The more I poured out my gratitude while sitting in my little Suzuki Swift, the more I felt at peace within myself. God was working for me and within me. I realised that it had taken a lead up to messy moments like this for me to highlight the goodness and faithfulness of my God. When I spoke those words into life, my actions started to align with what I was praying and after a few short moments, I couldn't help but laugh and smile because I just knew Jesus was with me – and He really was. He was there when I was a sobbing mess and He was also there when I made the choice to rejoice in the heartache. He had never left me and it became evident at that moment. Hannah Hurnard says it in a way that speaks volumes:

'One thing I can do radiantly and gladly is: to go through each day praising for everything that happens. For the disappointments as well as the joys. For disappointments accepted with praise always seem to turn into extra-radiant blessings.'[7]

---

7   Hannah Hurnard, 'Hinds' Feet On High Places', *Tyndale House Publishers Inc.*, p. 274

We can choose to go through life never acknowledging God, being fussy with what we praise Him for, or we can simply choose to be thankful for every little thing. When we choose to be grateful in times of pain, we realise that even the temporary disappointments are blessings in disguise.

Even When It Hurts (Hillsong Worship) is one of those songs where it really hits you right in the core. Especially that part in the live version when the lead singer, Taya, screams "I will only sing your praise" and you really feel the emotion behind it (if you haven't heard the song, please do yourself a favour and have a listen to it… It's too good not to know). I remember the early stages of dealing with the break up and cranking that song on the highest volume in the car. Everything inside of me could relate to every word that was being sung. I'm pretty sure the person at the stop light thought I was a mental case by how invested I was in singing this song, but at that moment I didn't even care how I looked. I was a total mess, tears and all, singing at the top of my lungs, while crying to myself "I FEEL YOUR PAIN. YOU BETTER SAAANG THAT GURL". If you've ever heard the lyrics, I bet you can relate to the visual imagery of how much of a mess I really looked. Every time I hear her sing those words, I still get goose bumps. In all my frustration and hurt, the declaration of only singing His praises and still choosing to lift Him up amidst all the craziness is what we can spiritually draw our strength from. I can testify to this. I had never felt refueled in God as much as I did when I would praise Him, thank Him and just acknowledge how good He was. Even on my hardest days. The more we try to strive on our own, the more we'll wear ourselves out. The more we submit to Him, while giving praise and gratitude, the more we will feel spiritually strengthened and be able to experience the peace and freedom that only He can offer.

In a time where it could have been so easy to blame God instead of honouring Him, I'm glad He was able to open up my heart to a place of gratitude. For others, it may not be entirely easy to thank God in the midst of a trial and I can completely understand where they are coming from. There were days where I felt like I could barely handle the emotional turmoil within myself, but it was on those days where breaking out of my comfort zone to praise and honour Him all the more was the only thing that helped me get through. Every time I would feel disheartened I would remember that there was a purpose to everything I was experiencing and that I wouldn't feel this way forever. This gave me reason to lift Him up all the more. During that time, I would be reminded of something I had read in Ann Voskamp's book 'The Broken Way':

HONEST SURRENDER

'Who knows why God allows heartbreak, but the answer must be important enough because God allows His heart to break too.'[8]

I had never really looked at it from the perspective of God because being caught up in the moment and thinking about how I was feeling was usually what came naturally, but how eye opening when we realise how much it also affects God. When we go through pain, we're not the only ones who suffer; His heart for us breaks too. Like a parent having to discipline their child for their wrongdoings and not necessarily enjoying the process of doing so is similar to how God's heart would ache by seeing us go through pain, yet knowing it's for our benefit. He only desires the best for us and sometimes in our stubbornness, we don't always see things the way He does. As we go through life, we will always be experiencing new learning curves, but regardless of what step we take, carrying an attitude of gratitude and praising Him in our weaknesses will go a long way in understanding that true joy and peace can only be found in Him alone.

---

8   Ann Voskamp, 'The Broken Way', *William K. Jensen Literary Agency*, p. 55

SEVEN

Be Okay

Have you ever worked yourself up to do something and then just as you're about to do that thing, you change your mind and end up backing out because of fear? Then you allow that fear to become a habit, to the point where it becomes second nature every time you think of doing the same thing? That can sometimes be us in our surrendering to God. We tell ourselves, "Okay God, this is the day I'm going to give it all to you. I've read books on it, I've prayed, I've worshipped, I'm ready to give it all up". But just as you're about to give it all to Him, a sudden fear of the future hits you, or you become fearful of letting a person go because you can't imagine what life would look like without them. As well as pride, fear is another one of the factors that tries to make its way in so that you're left giving into it. If fear were a person, I imagine them to be the kind of person who lives off of you, never contributes to the bills, never pays the rent, eats all the food and uses up all the electricity, yet still makes you feel like you need them around. How do we benefit from fear being a part of our life? We don't benefit at all! Fear doesn't do anything for us. It takes from us, belittles us and makes us feel like we are incapable. However, God tells us otherwise

2 Timothy 1:7 AMP
For God did not give us a spirit of timidity or cowardice or fear, but [He has given us a spirit] of power and of love and of sound judgment and personal discipline [abilities that result in a calm, well-balanced mind and self-control].

God also shows us that perfect love casts out all fear.

1 John 4:18 AMP
There is no fear in love [dread does not exist]. But perfect (complete, full-grown) love drives out fear, because fear involves [the expectation of divine] punishment, so the one who is afraid [of God's judgment]

is not perfected in love [has not grown into a sufficient understanding of God's love].

The more time we spend with God, the deeper we fall in love with Him. The deeper we fall in love, the more we trust Him, and the more we trust Him, the more we naturally surrender to His ways, allowing no opportunity for fear to linger.

It takes courage to be able to surrender. It takes boldness to be able to step out into new territory. Some people are great at change and some people struggle with the concept of change. No matter where we are headed in life, change is inevitable. The real challenge is more so *how* we will deal with the change. There can be situations where we step out with complete confidence and experience no fear of what may come, simply surrendering it all to God and taking on what the next journey entails, OR there can be situations where we step out fearing what's to come, yet still choose to surrender to God's will anyway. Out of the two, I was the latter. It took a lot of courage and a step at a time to fully surrender my thoughts and my ways to God. I didn't know what the future for me held now that Alexi was no longer there, but the more time I spent with God, the more I was able to give my honest surrender. I did eventually come to a point where I was okay with whether I ended up with Alexi or not, when before the thought of losing him would completely shatter me emotionally and mentally. Fear no longer held the reigns in my heart when I thought about my future. I found rest in knowing God had it all under control and it all stemmed from recognising the fear and finding the courage to overcome it through God's help. I never could have done it all on my own — the willingness to take a risk in the face of pain would have made fear feel the sense of itself. No longer was I going to let fear take a grip on me anymore; I had made a bold decision to take a stand against it. Ultimately the choice to leave fear led me to this simple reminder: God's love shows us that there is always a way out and it's through His grace that we are able to be guided through.

There were many times I was fearful of my future, but I remember one particular time during the break up where it almost felt unbearable. I questioned God and felt so unsure of myself, but throughout my doubts, God continued to comfort me. He constantly reminded me that He would never leave and He was always true to His Word.

Journal Entry - 12/8/18

I cried again. I realised that there's still so much that God wants to do in my heart during this process. I even listened to 'Even When It Hurts' for the thousandth time this week. One of the hardest and scariest parts about everything is not knowing when to let go. Where is the balance in that??? I'm constantly asking God for guidance and a solution, but at the same time it's just so difficult. At the end of the day I just need to give it back to God, because this burden is too hard to carry on my own. I guess Kelly helped me see it in another way; one of the toughest things to learn is how to give someone space despite how much it hurts us to wait and not know the outcome. This is a lesson in doing what's best for him, despite what it costs me. I just pray that God would take every part of this and have His way. To give me guidance, courage, peace and strength to see beyond the natural eye. Letting go of Alexi is one of the hardest things I've ever had to do, but if he ever does find his way back to me, at least I'll know it'll be out of God's heart and not my own human doing. Choosing to live righteously isn't always easy, but it's where true life is found.

It's currently summer in Australia (Amen for that) and so a couple of friends and I decided to go to the beach to swim, relax and get a nice golden tan. It was a little hotter than the weather forecast had informed us (the standard for Adelaide weather), but since we all had a day off, we decided to make the most of it. After our beach trip and over the next few days, I started to notice that the mole on my back (which I previously didn't give too much attention to in the past) had become increasingly itchy. I didn't think too much of it at first, but after a while, it felt as if the mole had raised from the skin and became a little bigger and lighter from what it used to resemble. I didn't know if it was just me over-thinking and being paranoid, but after remembering it had been exposed directly under the sun from our beach trip, it made me worry a little more than I usually would, so I decided to get it checked just in case. To be honest, I don't know a whole lot about moles, but I do know that some can be cancerous and since I had been directly under the sun for a long period of time, I mentally panicked and assumed the worst. I booked an appointment for the doctor to make sure it wasn't anything too serious and what a relief it was to hear from his mouth that it was a 'benign' mole, meaning the mole was harmless.

My doctor reassured me that it wasn't anything to worry about and since he had been my doctor for years, I simply took his word for it. He hadn't ever failed me in the past and his prescriptions and medical advice had always seemed to help, so it left me no room to doubt. From then on I didn't worry about the mole and still to this day, the mole hasn't caused me any harm. It still seems completely fine. Who knew a story about a mole could sound so dramatic. Now, If we're able to put our trust towards relieving us of fear in a person, whether that be a doctor, friend, family member, mentor, teacher, lawyer, etc. then how much *more* can we trust that God and His Word will never fail us? Worry can seep into our minds in the most inconvenient and vulnerable moments, but when we are constantly checking in with our Father, His reassurance overrides the doubt and fear that tries to settle in. When God tells us to put our faith and trust in Him, (similar to being able to trust my doctor's medical advice), we just have to take His word for it, despite what our surroundings around us may resemble. By recognising how much He loves us and trusting in Him, we give no leeway for fear to settle within us.

Imagine never being able to smell the outside fresh air, to never walk amongst a beautiful garden or experience walking barefoot on the sand alongside a picturesque view of the ocean, all because you were too afraid to step outside. This is how we can view God's promises for our lives sometimes. We can spiritually and mentally contain ourselves in fear, so much so that it distorts our trust in Him and it stops us from experiencing the beauty of what He wants to show us. We can miss out on all the incredible opportunities, simply because we are stuck in a fearful state of mind. There are many people in The Bible who demonstrate fearlessness in such a powerful way and of these people, Esther is one who clearly comes to mind.

Esther was chosen by God to use her influence in position to bring glory to God. She was a strong, courageous and remarkably fearless woman, who was even willing to risk her own life for what she truly believed in. If you don't know a lot about the book of Esther, here's a quick summary for you: The Persian King (King Xerxes) is looking for a wife so he pretty much creates the olden day version of 'The Bachelor' and selects a wife amongst the candidates presented to him. Apart from being highly favoured, Esther catches his eye with how beautiful she is and is eventually chosen by King Xerxes to become his Queen. Haman, who was honoured as one of the high officials of the King, was offended by Mordecai, (Esther's cousin) refusing to bow to him, so he decided he wanted to not only kill Moredecai (who is a Jew) for not complying, but also every other Jew (Haman, clearly a drama queen at its finest). Eventually an order gets sent out for every Jew to be destroyed, killed and annihilated. This is where Esther steps in to intercede and makes the bold choice to save her people, even at the cost of her own life.

Esther 4:16 AMP

Go, gather all the Jews that are present in Susa, and observe a fast for me; do not eat or drink for three days, night or day. I and my maids also will fast in the same way. Then I will go in to [see] the king [without being summoned], which is against the law; and if I perish, I perish.

Without the King's consent, she approaches King Xerxes' inner court and requests to throw a banquet for him and Haman. The King accepts her request and it is at the banquet, where Esther fearlessly pleads for her people's life, as well as her own and the King grants her appeal. Haman's plan to kill Mordecai and the other Jews ends up failing and the original order sent out to destroy all Jews was cancelled. The King then orders for Haman to be hung, leaving the lives of all Jews to be spared. It was Esther's act of bravery and fearlessness that highly contributed to saving the lives of many that day. Her story teaches us to break the power of intimidation that the enemy tries to scare us with and ultimately see God's promises come to pass.

Another exceptional example of fearlessness is the story of Ruth the Moabite, who despite losing her husband, chose to follow his mother into unknown territories.

Ruth 1:16-17 AMP
But Ruth said, "Do not urge me to leave you or to turn back from following you; for where you go, I will go, and where you lodge, I will lodge. Your people will be my people, and your God, my God. Where you die, I will die, and there I will be buried. May the Lord do the same to me [as He has done to you], and more also, if anything but death separates me from you."

To summarize, Ruth's obedience and fearless nature allowed her to meet her future husband (Boaz), eventually being blessed with a son (Obed - a grandson Naomi was able to care for after losing her two sons), who was also part of the lineage of Jesus. Her act of fearlessness not only brought favour for her own life, but for the generations to come. What an inspiring way to live and what an encouraging example for us to follow. Our simple act of stepping out in confidence and fearlessness not only affects us, but directly affects those in close proximity to us and eventually the generations to come.

Jesus Himself lived a fearless life, knowing that one day He would need to sacrifice His life to save the lives of many. People denying Him and treating Him unfairly would have been enough to try to avoid the situation. Jesus also struggled with the idea of sacrifice, as we see in Luke 22:42 AMP, saying:

> *"Father, if You are willing, remove this cup [of divine wrath] from Me; yet not My will, but [always] Yours be done."*

Remember, He walked on the earth as a human too. Despite all of this, Jesus filled with immense compassion for the people, *still* decided to follow through with His Father's plan. By living out what His Heavenly Father planned and accomplishing what was needed to be done, Jesus chose to free us so that we too can live a fearless life in Him.

As we have seen with the examples of Esther, Ruth and Jesus Himself (as well as many other people who are in The Bible), living a fearless life can be such a big step to take. It requires boldness, faith, selflessness and sacrifice, all of which can seem rather overwhelming. However, when we take into consideration our Heavenly Father, who stands *with us* during these times, as well as the goodness we see from making such a large decision, not to mention how much it accomplishes for His Kingdom, it's not as overpowering and frightening as the enemy makes it out to be.

EIGHT

Lean Back

Looking back on everything I've gone through, I can confidently say that I'm grateful for the heartache God allowed me to experience. I have learnt to be resilient and it's because of these hardships I had to face along the way. His ways are better than I could've ever imagined and all it really takes is for us to lean on God, because He already knows the outcome.

Proverbs 3:5-6 AMP
Trust in and rely confidently on the Lord with all your heart and do not rely on your own insight or understanding. In all your ways know

and acknowledge and recognize Him, and He will make your paths straight and smooth [removing obstacles that block your way].

That's not to say that I still don't experience hardships now… They're just different to what I had to deal with before. In that season of my life, God was revealing to me the issues in my heart and ungodly attitudes that needed to be purged by His grace before I could be accelerated into the plans He has in store for me. He has taught me and better equipped me to be aware of how I respond to difficult situations that may arise and He can do the same for you. Ultimately, we can't change our past and if we live in regret, it will only keep us from living out the complete freedom God desires for us. Let's choose to allow our present selves to bask in God's joy today and when you do, you'll notice a change in the way you experience life.

When we're younger, we're told by our parents not to do certain things and if we cross the line, we're disciplined for them. My siblings and I loved to create amusement out of dull moments. We loved to entertain ourselves with fun ideas (also considered as dangerous and life threatening) and hyped one another so much that we would actually go through with them. One of these ideas got us into huge trouble and we got what was coming for us when our parents found out. When we were younger, we lived in a two-storey house and the upstairs window made it easy for us to access the roof of the verandah, which overlooked the backyard. As kids, we thought it would be a genius idea to jump down from the verandah's roof onto the concrete floor either barefoot or with slippers on. Bear in mind the roof was actually quite high, so it was pretty dangerous, but from a kid's perspective, it was all in good fun and adventure. As kids we didn't take into account what could happen if we accidentally landed the wrong way, how painful it would be if we did, the ambulance expenses that our parents would have to deal with if anything bad went wrong, as well as how they would feel knowing their children were in pain.

In our childish minds, we simply wanted to feel the adrenaline rush and have fun. We started off by just jumping off the verandah roof, until one of us suggested that we needed to use garbage bags as 'parachutes' (knowing us, it was probably my eldest sister's idea) because we would feel like we were flying. Needless to say, it didn't go the way we had intended. You could imagine what our parents had to say and what they did when they found out what we had been doing behind their back. Being Filipino parents, their discipline was quite harsh and in hindsight I'm glad that they dealt with it in a way that made us remember not to act so recklessly again. In light of that example, isn't that what we can be like sometimes? We make our own decisions, not taking into account the consequences it may bring for our future. We entertain certain mentalities and thoughts, choosing our own ideas over what God wants for us. We reason and decide that our way is better than His. It's our childish mentality of only wanting what's in the moment that selfishly takes and takes from the honest surrender we could be investing in God. All in all, God knows best; He knows what's already going to happen before we make decisions, He sees it all. We aren't fooling anyone but ourselves when we try to convince Him otherwise.

All throughout life, we are constantly growing, changing and adapting. We are given free choice in life and since none of us are perfect, of course we're going to stuff up at some point. It's inevitable that we'll make mistakes, but those mistakes give us opportunities to learn some valuable lessons that usually teach and propel us towards the next steps of what God has planned for our lives. Like I had mentioned before, our Heavenly Father always knows best. His best isn't there to prove a point and to show us how stupid we can be (because I for one can vouch for some dumb decisions I've made in the past). Instead He leads and teaches us to become more Christ-like in how we respond to difficulties, simply because He loves us. Because of our mistakes, we are able to truly recognise how gracious and sovereign our Father really is. He is in complete authority over everything and yet in our disobedience, rather than striking us down right then and there, through The Holy Spirit, we are continuously encouraged and prompted to follow His ways. It's in those defining moments while enduring a trial where our character is truly tested. His intention is never to condemn us or to make us feel inadequate. Instead He desires to fill us with His love, mercy and grace so that we feel safe even in the midst of the hurt, reminding us that He is the answer to all things and nothing else can suffice. Our Heavenly Father stops at nothing to see us reach our full potential in Him; that is if we choose to give ourselves over to Him completely.

When I look at all the past decisions I've made and how inconsiderate I was towards God's heart, I'm amazed at the fact that He still stood by me. It blows me away when I think of how much He really loves us and yet I will never understand the depth of His love. As people we make mistakes time and time again and yet He chooses to forgive us in an instant just because He loves us. How many times can we say we've forgiven someone who has hurt us intensely, in an instant? Usually it takes time for us to even adapt to the idea of forgiveness, but our Father chooses to love us with no limits, because He *is* love.

1 John 4:8 AMP

The one who does not love has not become acquainted with God [does not and never did know Him], for God is love. [He is the originator of love, and it is an enduring attribute of His nature.]

While looking through my old journals, I came across a letter I had written to God while dealing with the break up. I still remember the intense gratitude I felt as I wrote it, but most importantly, amidst the pain, I remember a complete sense of God's sustaining love.

Letter to God - 31/7/18

God, you are just so so good to me. You've taught me what it means to truly love and forgive, even when I least deserve it. When I found it hard to forgive myself, you willingly came to my aid. In my stumbling, you picked me up and reminded me that you are the way. In the moments where I felt defeated, you found me and commissioned hope. When life looked dark and the silence felt inescapable, your word was my song that I held onto. Your love was and is unfailing; a love that is incomparable to anything I've ever experienced, a love that I cling to and could never question the motive. Despite my brokenness, you remained by my side; You called me home, when I tried so hard to run from you. Despite my mess, your infinite love saw the ugliest parts of me and yet you still decided that I was worthy of your attention. Although I may never be able to fully express the gratitude and love I have, with what I do have to give, I hope to continue showing others what you have taught me. All this to say, I will never look through the lens of life the same. I now have a deeper understanding of extending grace to others, because of the unreserved grace you willingly gave me.

I remember the first book I read after my break up. It was called 'Redeeming Love' by Francine Rivers. I was recommended this book by a couple of friends who had gone through a similar journey and since I loved reading and needed to keep my mind off of the situation, I decided to read the book. In fact, it was gifted to me from a sweet friend of mine who believed I would really appreciate it. If I had known the array of emotions I'd feel while reading that book, I would have somehow better prepared myself. My heart was not equipped for the emotions that came with the reading at all. I was never a big 'crier' when it came to books, but let me tell you, when I read Redeeming Love, my ugly crying evolved into something else. That book had me a sobbing mess. I had to take so many moments to just pause and allow my tears to come, because I completely related to most of what I read in the story. Francine Rivers bases the story on the book of Hosea in The Bible and writes from the back and forth perspective of the prostitute (Angel) and Michael, the man pursuing her. Michael, who is in pursuit of Angel, represents Jesus and how He relentlessly chases us down with His love. In short, It's a beautiful story of Jesus' sustaining love and endless grace for us, despite our messiness. As I read these specific words in the book, I remember crying for a long while. It was as if God was directly speaking into my heart and reminding me that through the wait of the pain, casting blame on myself was not part of what He wanted for me. His sustaining love was there for me to take a complete hold of. Francine Rivers wrote it so beautifully:

"Love cleanses, beloved. It doesn't beat you down. It doesn't cast blame." He kissed her again, wishing he had the right words to say what he felt. Words would never be enough to show her what he meant. "My love isn't a weapon. It's a lifeline. Reach out and take hold, and don't let go."[9]

The more love I felt from God, the more I was able to pour out onto those around me. His grace and compassion for me became a grace and compassion I willingly gave to others. He was teaching me all that He was and because I had surrounded myself with Him daily, it simply became a part of who I was. This is what God desires of us: that we would be so immersed and in love with who He is that it actually becomes who we are. Although we may never fully reflect the perfection of who Jesus is in one hit, we can aim to become more like Him everyday. Out of these reminders, I had

---

9 Francine Rivers, 'Redeeming Love', *Multnomah Books - an imprint of The Crown Publishing Group*, p. 292

written a poem on how God's love found me at one of my weakest moments and I remember thinking to myself how lost I would be without His sustaining love.

> *I found a love; the kind that doesn't seep through the cracks, the kind that overflows with passion; one of warmth and depth. I found this love at my weakest, which makes me wonder. If I were at my weakest, with no strength left to bear; it must have been this love who found me instead.*

How incredible that God's persevering love can continue to transform us daily. Although I'm still learning, He continues to teach me to love others in a way that disregards their faults and chooses to look past their mistakes. His love brings us to a place of sincere and honest surrender and that is one of the most fulfilling places to be.

NINE

Heart Of God

As I'm writing this chapter, I'm also thinking about how I still need to buy Christmas presents for my loved ones (multitasking at its finest) because Christmas is exactly 20 days away… 20. Days. Away. People. How did the time go by so fast?! This is honestly the ongoing question of my life. No matter what day of the year or month it is, somehow there is always so much to think about and do in such a small amount of time and for some of us, we want to get it done all at once. Realistically, we usually have to spread tasks out over the day (even weeks or months depending on what it is) and that requires a lot of patience on our end. We think we have it hard by having to juggle work, time with friends, family, church, a social life etc. but imagine how God feels having to deal with the rest of us, with us always on the go, asking for things, expecting things, complaining about anything and everything… We never give Him a break! Not that He needs one anyway because after all, He is God, but what I admire about His nature is that on top of the craziness that is our lives, He still *chooses* to be patient with us.

Part of my honest surrender in the season where I had to deal with forgiveness in myself and choosing to prioritise God again was learning to be patient. I'm a natural organiser and prefer things planned ahead of time, so it was really difficult for me not to have a back up plan. God had to be my everything and so that meant His ways were the first plan and also the back up plan, even when I had no idea what was ahead of time. I imagine that if I were to be over my own life, things definitely would not have turned out the way they do now, that's for sure. During that time, I do remember God specifically speaking to me about learning patience and in order for me to grasp a hold of honest surrender, He needed to teach me how to wait well.

I recall one time I was listening to a Steven Furtick sermon and God had already shown me a verse that I hadn't looked into too much, but when it came up again on his sermon, I knew He was trying to get my attention. The verse was found in Romans 8:25 AMP:

> *"But if we hope for what we do not see, we wait eagerly for it with patience and composure."*

I realised that although I was waiting, the time within the waiting wasn't there for me to wait for the sake of just waiting (tongue twister I know), but God was wanting me to make use of my time with "patience and composure". When I think of patience, I relate it to self-discipline and a sense of calmness. When I think of composure, I relate this to self-assurance and confidence. In this waiting season of my life, God was wanting me to become self-disciplined when it came to making certain choices, while having a confident assurance in Him. I came to a realisation that I actually needed to be productive while waiting and for some people that can be challenging. This gives us the question to consider: what does productive waiting look like for us? Below we see how people in The Bible were able to put their trust in God throughout their period of waiting and what they did in order to wait well.

Noah was a great example of somebody who had spent a very long time being productive in his wait, eventually having his life, his family's life and the animals in the ark spared from the labours of his patience and composure. We see this in the way he built the ark for God. Noah didn't just build any ark, God was very particular with the instructions on *how* to build the ark.

Genesis 6:15-16 NIV
This is how you are to build it: The ark is to be three hundred cubits long, fifty cubits wide and thirty cubits high. Make a roof for it, leaving below the roof an opening one cubit high all around. Put a door in the side of the ark and make lower, middle and upper decks.

That in itself demonstrates extraordinary patience and self-discipline. Noah had to pay careful attention to God's words and follow them precisely. Something I admire about Noah's response to what God asked of him was that he did *everything* as God commanded him, showing that he was confident in what God was asking of him.

Genesis 6:22 NIV
Noah did everything just as God commanded him.

He didn't add or leave anything out and he didn't question God or doubt His ways. He simply followed God's orders and went to work. I don't doubt for a second that people would have looked at what Noah was doing and believed him to be a madman, building an ark and not understanding what the purpose of it was, yet even still, he disregarded what others thought of him and remained faithful to God.

Similar to our lives, your waiting season may look different to everyone else and it may not always make sense in the moment (whether that be to you or others), but don't let your external surroundings affect the time it takes you to work on yourself with God. Whether God has given you specific instructions on your wait, or not a lot to work with, choose to be obedient and trust Him in the process. When the flood came, Noah's life, his family's life and the animals inside the ark were spared, all because of his patience, obedience and trust in God. He worked hard to build that ark, as well as being patient in doing so and it had such a significant purpose to fulfill. This is the same for our own lives. During the wait, our character is being strengthened as we lean on His ways. Eventually we will see how crucial it is to be faithful in the waiting moments, as we continue to fulfill all that He has for our lives.

Someone who exemplified extraordinary patience and composure in such a gracious and Godly way was Hannah. Personally, I've never been in a position to wait on conceiving a child and I could only imagine how frustrating and discouraging it would be to have suffered in this situation, but Hannah held herself together with poised determination. Hannah not only waited years and years to bear a son, but she also had to deal with Peninnah (Elkanah's second wife), who continued to provoke her during this time. After years of Hannah crying out to God and continuing to worship Him, she was finally able to conceive.

1 Samuel 1:20 AMP
It came about in due time, after Hannah had conceived, that she gave birth to a son; she named him Samuel, saying, "Because I have asked for him from the Lord."

Looking at Hannah's response, there are a couple of things that are very admirable in regards to how she handled her waiting season. Hannah had a rival who stopped at nothing to pull her down, made her feel like she was incapable and unable to fulfill her duty as a woman.

1 Samuel 1:6-7 AMP
Hannah's rival provoked her bitterly, to irritate and embarrass her, because the Lord had left her childless. So it happened year after year, whenever she went up to the house of the Lord, Peninnah provoked her; so she wept and would not eat.

Doesn't this sound similar to what the enemy does to us? He will do anything he can to make us feel worthless and incapable of fulfilling all that God has planned for our lives, but while the enemy attempts to taunt us and bring us down, rather than giving in and listening to his lies, we can use this as a way to fight back by holding firm onto our faith and continuing to pray to our Father. Be encouraged that your waiting is never done in vain and similar to Hannah, who eventually conceived after countless years of seeking after God in prayer, you will also see your promises come to pass in due time.

Hannah never gave up on seeing the promise come to life. She was persistent and passionate in the way she prayed. We see this in 1 Samuel 1:10-11 AMP:

> *Hannah was greatly distressed, and she prayed to the Lord and wept in anguish. She made a vow, saying, "O Lord of hosts, if You will indeed look on the affliction (suffering) of Your maidservant and remember, and not forget Your maidservant, but will give Your maidservant a son, then I will give him to the Lord all the days of his life; a razor shall never touch his head.*

During our wait, God is looking for a fervency in our prayers; a genuine desire for more of Him and to seek out His presence.

Prayer keeps us productive in our wait and every word we speak is precious to our Father.

When Hannah gave birth to Samuel and he was at a reasonable age, she kept her vow by choosing to dedicate him to God, allowing him to serve under Eli the priest in the temple.

1 Samuel 1:27-28 AMP
For this child I prayed, and the Lord has granted me my request which I asked of Him. Therefore I have also dedicated him to the Lord; as long as he lives he is dedicated to the Lord." And they worshiped the Lord there.

What an astounding act of obedience and sacrifice. She had prayed for so long, waited for her miracle to come and yet she was still willing to give him back to God with complete joy and thanksgiving in her heart. (Shown in 1 Samuel 2:1-10). This shows how pure Hannah's intentions were towards God and one we ourselves can learn from. In the season of waiting, God is able to test the intentions of our hearts. He desires for us to reflect His very heart by removing all factors of selfishness and self-seeking behaviour. Our season of waiting is able to produce complete reliance in God, knowing that whatever He chooses to give us and bless us with after the wait can easily be surrendered back to Him if need be. Ultimately, it's not necessarily about what we are waiting for (whether that be a relationship, a job, or another type of answer to prayer), but it's about the pure intentions of our hearts and allowing the strength of character that God has developed in us during the wait, to propel us into understanding what it truly means to surrender. For my own life, I remember coming to the conclusion that whether Alexi and I ended up together or not, it wouldn't change how I viewed God and it wouldn't change how much I was willing to seek and surrender to Him. I would continue to worship Him in every moment and do so with a heart of joy and thanksgiving because I understood who He is and who He has always been. It wasn't about expecting to receive anything back from Him, but simply resting in the assurance that He is good regardless of the outcome.

When I think of Hannah and her bold faith, courageous strength and consistent trust in The Father, I'm reminded of my eldest sister, Krishelle. As I write this, just three days ago, something unexpected happened that shook mine and my family's world. It was so sudden and a complete shock to us all. Thinking of how my family is continuing to grieve over such a mournful loss, yet having God as our cornerstone, as well as supportive friends and loving family has helped us stay strong. I had never felt pain this deep before and for anyone who has ever lost a loved one so suddenly, they too would understand the extreme heartbreak of it all. It was three days ago where my eldest sister, Krishelle was told that her baby had no heartbeat and that she would still have to give birth to her daughter. As an aunty I'm completely devastated and having to deal with the anguish and the pain, which has been overwhelming for me, but as a mother and a father, I could only imagine how my sister and my brother-in-law would be feeling; having waited for so long to finally hold their child in their arms, only to have her sleep forever.

After seeing a photo of her sweet little face and her rosy lips, it kicked back into reality that this perfect little newborn was here physically, but her spirit was now with God. I wasn't prepared for this kind of news when we were told and it was in that painful few seconds where my heart instantly dropped. As a family, we had anticipated her arrival and after the prolonged wait, our excitement quickly turned into sorrow. I cried heavy tears that night, with Alexi comforting me as best he could, although I could see that he too was in deep pain. We were all hurting; our hearts were completely battered and bruised. It was at that moment I knew God's heart was breaking for us too. What made my insides pierce even more is that my little nephew of three and niece of six had to be informed of the news on the night of her delivery. The thought of their innocent, sweet selves being told that their baby sister, who they had sung to, prayed for and eagerly waited so long to meet was no longer here, is completely shattering in itself. How I admire my eldest sister, Krishelle and brother-in-law, Jude, to have still held tightly onto the promises of God, despite losing their beautiful baby daughter, Sierra Rose Galang.

For the two of them to stand firm and trust that God still had everything in control, regardless of the external circumstances, has been such an inspiration to many, including myself and I've watched how even in times of hurt and confusion, they have grounded themselves in Him alone; how they have spoken so highly of our Father and given Him complete glory. Their attitude towards giving the situation wholly to God is the epitome of honest surrender, leading their family in a season of complete heartache and pain to the only light that can provide peace, comfort and strength in a time as difficult as this. My family and I immediately caught a plane to Sydney to be with them and in the few days we were all present, our bond grew deeper, allowing us all to become closer than we had ever been. Looking on from everything that has happened since, I've come to understand that maybe we will never know the reasons why Sierra was taken so soon and maybe it's not for us to ever know, but I have seen God's light amidst the suffering and it was through her passing where once again we were all reminded of the importance of family and togetherness. Rather than having our intentions be hateful towards God, we are able to appreciate one another more than we ever have. As a family, we are still grieving, but we have the assurance and are comforted by the glorious fact that our little Sierra is now safe in the arms of our loving Father.

In Chapter Five, I mentioned how my relationship with Alexi was affected three months out from our wedding due to past struggles being resurfaced. Although that time of our life took much reliance on God and we found our healing in Him, we were also hit with another challenge and were once again faced with patience. As if it wasn't a long enough wait already: dating for four years, breaking up for a few months, getting back together for another year and then finally getting engaged, we hoped it would be an eleven month engagement, only to be forced to postpone our wedding due to a world pandemic (COVID-19) and having to extend the wait even longer. I will always be grateful that God had taken us on a waiting journey beforehand because He was able to prepare us mentally, emotionally, physically and spiritually for the season we had ahead. Looking back, I still remember hoping we would get married on the day we had planned, but knowing that however it turned out, God was still good and in control. Amidst all the uncertainty, we stayed confident in His promise and trusted that His ways were better than our own. Alexi and I were able to take our eyes off the things we didn't have and humbly thank Him for everything we did have.

For our own lives, we may never understand the reasons why things happen the way they do and although our wait may feel like precious time has been wasted, it never changes the fact that God is *still* faithful and *still* good in all circumstances. He has a purpose in all that He allows and as we ourselves go through the challenges of everyday life, maybe one day we too will look back and cherish the moments we once fought so hard to understand.

One of the most difficult parts about waiting is that at times you can feel like God isn't there, or that He has left you when you need Him the most, but this is never the case and couldn't be further from the truth. Wendy Pope writes:

'God is never inactive or unresponsive when it comes to His children. He is always working. When God appears to be silent or sedentary, lean closer and press in harder, but never believe He doesn't see or hear your cries.'[10]

During my time of learning to be patient in Him, there were many instances where I felt unsure of what to do next, but the more I pressed into God, the more at peace I felt. It didn't automatically mean I knew where to go from there; it just made me

---

10   Wendy Pope, 'Wait And See', *David C Cook*, p. 198

more aware of the fact that it didn't matter whether or not I had received an answer right then and there. Knowing He was with me was enough for me to continue the wait. Ultimately, God knows what's best for us and He doesn't have to prove Himself any more than He already has. All we need to do on our end is trust in the waiting process and put our assured confidence in Him, regardless of what we see and feel naturally.

TEN

To Worship You I Live

As I had mentioned in the preceding chapters, in early womanhood, I never really liked the idea of being 'accountable' and I didn't want to feel like I was being controlled by God or by others in the way I made decisions and lived my life. For so long I tried to do things my own way, until I finally realised that by relying on myself, I was actually being controlled by my own emotions and fears. This was causing me to spiral down and made me doubt myself. I understood that emotions were a normal part of humanity because God Himself created them, but to be *controlled by them* was another issue on its own. I was manipulated by the enemy to believe I had known better, but thank God, He showed me a greater way.

In an article regarding emotions, Jon Bloom writes, 'God designed your emotions to be gauges, not guides. They're meant to report to you, not dictate you.'[11] Emotions aren't there to be our deciding point on how we deal with a particular person or situation, but they're there to give us an idea of *how* something is affecting us, ultimately directing us to draw closer to God for guidance and as our number one source. He is the only one who knows the outcome to every situation. Whether it seems like a big deal or a small one, everything we do is best guided by giving it over to God. Over the years, I've noticed there has been speculation over God being in control. When we give things over to Him, this can be easily misinterpreted as God 'controlling' our lives and us having no say or freedom. I used to have a similar mentality about this concept, until I caught a revelation of who He really is and actually experienced first hand all the goodness He had in store for me when I chose to surrender.

Imagine being stuck in terrible traffic and you're in a rush to get to where you need to because you're already late, but the traffic

---

11 [Online] Available at: https://www.desiringgod.org/articles/your-emotions-are-a-gauge-not-a-guide [Accessed 9th December, 2019]

light has just turned orange (which obviously means to slow down). You have two choices in that split second of a moment. You can choose to go against the law, risk driving through a red light, possibly getting a fine for doing so, as well as risking hurting yourself and other drivers, OR you could choose to slow down and wait until the traffic lights turn green to go. The obvious answer would be the safer one: to wait. But sometimes it can be tempting to just drive straight through, right? I know because I've been in this situation many times – literally and metaphorically. If we solely relied on our emotions and how we felt in that moment, I'm assuming a majority of us would probably choose to just go through the orange light while thinking to ourselves, "It doesn't hurt, it's just one time". But what if that one time turns into a habit? What if that one time you think you'll get away with it ends up turning into a hefty fine, or accidentally getting into a car accident? Now I know this is an extreme example, but isn't this how we deal with life sometimes? We can get ourselves into situations that are out of our control and if we make one wrong move based on the influence of our emotions as our main source, this increases the risk of only making things worse. Relying on how we feel in the moment isn't always the best source to be guided by. There are times where I absolutely cannot be bothered to get up for work and just want to lay in bed all day, but if I always followed through on how I felt at that moment, I would be letting myself down and letting my team at work down. Take another example: I get hungry ALL the time (this Filipino appetite is something else) and if I followed my feelings, I would literally eat anything and everything, but there are times when I have to discipline my appetite because craving to eat a fat schnitzel at 3:00am in the morning, and actually going through with it, is probably not the best option.

Knowing me, it could turn into a habit and that for sure would not go down well. What I'm basically trying to say is that our emotions are all over the place. Sure, you may be able to hold yourself together well in some cases, but we can't do that forever. As humans, we're flawed. We're impulsive, we make promises and don't always keep them. We let ourselves and others down. We're annoyed one minute and then happy the next. We can be inconsistent with how we feel, changing from one emotion to the next and that's why we aren't a completely reliable source just on our own. God on the other hand is constant and unchanging in His ways.

Malachi 3:6 AMP
For I am the Lord, I do not change [but remain faithful to My covenant with you]; that is why you, O sons of Jacob, have not come to an end.

If anything, He created us and knows us, even before we're born, so this gives us more reason to trust in the fact that any decision we make, even before we make it, is already known by our Creator. He simply guides us on the right path, if we give Him that permission to do so in our life. By having an understanding of this, we can have a peace and a large sense of stability in ourselves, knowing that we aren't alone. How comforting to know that our Father remains the same through everything and we can rely on Him in every aspect of life.

When I think of being in control of my own emotions, I think of the 'Choose Your Own Adventure' books. These were my favourite kind of books to read in my early high school years. I even used to make little versions of the 'Choose Your Own Adventure' books for my youngest sister. That's how much I loved them. For those of you who aren't familiar with these kind of books, let me give you a small rundown of how it works: You read through each chapter and at the end of it, you're given two choices. One choice usually leads you to a dead end of the story and the other one continues on. So for example, it would say: "Johnny walked by the abandoned house on Delaware Crescent and stopped as he noticed a cat by the upstairs window. Johnny, being a big cat lover, was torn between leaving the cat behind or taking it with him. The only thing was, if he did choose to bring the cat home, that would mean entering the house and who knows what he would find in there. If you choose for Johnny to leave the poor kitty behind, go to chapter 3. If you choose for Johnny to enter the old, spooky house, go to chapter 4".

What I always noticed in these books was how difficult the author made it for the reader to choose. Take the example I gave above for instance. If I choose to leave the 'poor kitty' behind, then it may lead me to a boring ending and I'd feel less like a hero. If I chose to enter the house to save the cat, then I would fulfill the hero's expectations and the story may get more interesting. I did find that sometimes even the more interesting choice I assumed would lead to more adventure was actually the choice that led to a dead end. Nevertheless, no matter what was chosen, it was always a risk and the reader was left in a difficult position to choose the option they felt was better. Similar to the 'Choose Your Own Adventure' books, sometimes in life we too can end up in challenging predicaments. We're left with questions like "Do I or don't I"?, "Should I or shouldn't I"? It's a continuous pull between what you want to do and what you know is right to do.

Romans 7:15-20 NLT
I don't really understand myself, for I want to do what is right, but I don't do it. Instead, I do what I hate. But if I know that what I am doing is wrong, this shows that I agree that the law is good. So I am

not the one doing wrong; it is sin living in me that does it. And I know that nothing good lives in me, that is, in my sinful nature. I want to do what is right, but I can't. I want to do what is good, but I don't. I don't want to do what is wrong, but I do it anyway. But if I do what I don't want to do, I am not really the one doing wrong; it is sin living in me that does it.

The good thing about giving over control to God is that He is already aware of the outcome. Although we go through the highs and lows, we can trust that the outcome will be just as He promised, as opposed to guessing if we will reach a dead end or not. God proves Himself to be faithful every time, even if that does require delays and challenges along the way.

Today, I was driving to work for my overnight shift and I was thinking about how the night before I was super-tired because my night owl mode decided to kick in a little more than usual and I didn't go to sleep the time I was initially planning to. This resulted in making me extra tired for my shift (well whose fault is that? I only blame myself) and all I wanted to do was drive back home, snuggle on the couch with my two cats, make myself a hot chai tea and watch a movie. Unfortunately, I snapped back into reality and I was about five minutes from the placement, dreading the night ahead. In fact, I'm writing this chapter at work because I have some extra time on my hands (I promise I do work ninety-five percent of the time… this is a one off occasion). What I realised was, although I wasn't feeling up for it, I still had a choice in how I would respond to the situation. I was still in control of my attitude towards it, despite how I was feeling. Then it dawned on me. I could easily mope around the workplace and bring down the mood because I felt too tired and frustrated that it wasn't my night in, but instead, I prayed to God to help me throughout the night and to not allow how I was feeling to dictate my mood, or how I acted during the shift. I chose to pray a simple prayer, which in turn changed my attitude and helped a lot with how I felt the rest of the night.

My clients and I actually had a nice, relaxing time and I was able to take a step back and be thankful for the job God had blessed me with. All it took was prayer and a willingness to change my attitude. I say this all for us to see that even in situations that seem small and insignificant, surrendering our emotions to God can make us realise that even these simple passing moments are worthy of His praise. For what could have been a night of just getting through work, actually turned into a realisation of how grateful I am for even being blessed with a job like this one and having the wonderful opportunity to spend time with the clients I have. Imagine having that same realisation of gratefulness every single day. If we're just willing to give God control of our emotions, then we too can experience each day (even the seemingly insignificant moments) as an extraordinary blessing.

Journaling was a method that really helped me deal with my emotions during the difficult break up season with Alexi. I have always been someone who loved the idea of all things written: poetry, letters, devotional journals, reading, noting etc. so writing a journal on how I was feeling each day made sense and really helped me put it all into perspective and process how I was feeling, without making my emotions the main focus and acting on them without thinking. God was able to speak to me through this approach and I found that the more I was able to express how I felt, the more freeing it was to then direct my attention to God for His comfort and peace. At the beginning of my emotional turmoil, I remember desiring to find a solution to everything all at once: from how I was feeling, to finding different ways in stopping the frustration and a whole heap of other things, such as wanting Alexi's pain to be at ease too. This is one of the many examples of situations I was trying to find solutions to that were purely out of my control, while figuring out how I would cope seeing him at church when we both led in the same campus and in the same team.

It drove me quite insane to be honest, but as I continued to put the unhealthy control of my emotions in God's hands and completely trusted in Him, I found that I stopped relying solely on the need to see natural progress take place or trying to discover a natural solution to these problems. Over time, I was reminded that Jesus *was* and *is* the solution, so everything that *is* drawn from Him and all that He was pouring out onto me was exactly what I needed to sustain me. This isn't to say that seeing natural progress is bad because that's not the case at all. It's only when we solely rely on wanting to see natural progress and natural solutions on their own that it becomes an issue because we then box in a *supernatural* God, who is capable of moving in more ways beyond our scope of understanding. When we choose to trust in His ways (ways that may not always be seen), we are exercising our God-given faith and this in itself is pleasing to our Father and allows for miracles to take place.

God never demands anything of us. In fact, He consistently encourages us, all the while waiting until we are ready to come to Him. In the previous chapters, I mentioned how we are given freedom in the decisions we make. When we truly grasp the revelation of how much God loves us and only wants what's best for our lives, we are drawn towards Him and it becomes *our choice*, in our own *free will*, to put God in control. Although it can sometimes be challenging to surrender the temptation to be led by our emotions, we can continue to make our requests known to God, so He can guide us in our struggles, ultimately leading to His peace.

Philippians 4:6-7 AMP
Do not be anxious or worried about anything, but in everything [every circumstance and situation] by prayer and petition with thanksgiving, continue to make your [specific] requests known to God. And the peace of God [that peace which reassures the heart, that peace] which transcends all understanding, [that peace which] stands guard over your hearts and your minds in Christ Jesus [is yours].

Part of our worship to God is giving Him control of our thoughts and emotions. This is part of our honest surrender and what it truly is to live a fulfilled life in Him.

ELEVEN

Grace To Grace

When you think of 'grace', what is the first thing that pops into your head? For some it may be a visual picture of Jesus dying on the cross, a huge sense of gratitude for past mistakes that were forgiven, or maybe even a mental picture of a gift being given to you, while for others it may have as little meaning (in comparison to the examples above) as a popular woman's name. When I think of God's grace, I'm humbled at how loved I am by Him and how He saw me as enough to not only send His son as a living sacrifice to atone for *our* sins, but how He continues to pour out His grace onto me even to this day.

Ephesians 2:4-5 AMP
But God, being [so very] rich in mercy, because of His great and wonderful love with which He loved us, even when we were [spiritually] dead and separated from Him because of our sins, He made us [spiritually] alive together with Christ (for by His grace—His undeserved favor and mercy—you have been saved from God's judgment).

I look back on some of the choices I've made growing up and despite my attitudes and mistakes, God still continued to look past them all while wanting me as I was. He had always been a Father patiently waiting for my heart, even in times when I was too stubborn to give it to Him. He has that same heart for us all today. It used to cause me much confusion when I'd think about the distinctions between mercy and grace, so in my younger days, I ended up just jumbling the two concepts into one meaning. It was only until I experienced them separately where I truly understood the difference between them and realised that they both carried significant meanings. So what is the difference between mercy and grace? Well, simply put, 'mercy is God *not giving* us what we *do* deserve, while grace is God *giving* us something we *do not* deserve.'¹² Let me take an example of my own life for instance: when I was younger, I would choose to go back to my old ways by continuously retreating to a toxic relationship in high school with my ex-boyfriend, who physically abused me over many years. However, God showed His *mercy* by saving me from that relationship and allowing me to not have any major life threatening injuries take place (due to the consistent physical abuse). He also showed me mercy by not striking me down right then and there for the stupidity of choosing that relationship over Him.

Although I put myself in these situations, God was merciful enough to save me from the pain, which could have escalated further. On the other hand, when I became older and Alexi and I broke up, God showed His *grace* by standing with us on our individual journeys, eventually mending the hurt in our relationship and bringing us back together. Although both of us had failed Him in our own ways, God was gracious enough to give our relationship a second chance. He demonstrated mercy and grace in separate ways, even though for so long I had tried to label them as one definition. As I look at how much God has extended His mercy and grace for me and those around me, I'm taken aback

---

12 [Online] Available at: https://www.compellingtruth.org/mercy-grace.html [Accessed 17th December, 2019]

with immense gratitude at the fact that He doesn't just stop there. His supply is endless, overflowing and He chooses to offer this to us daily.

It is God's sufficient grace that has been highlighted throughout my life and because of His grace, I was able to appreciate what He had done for me, causing me to make decisions towards living a life set apart and living with purpose.

2 Timothy 1:9 AMP
For He delivered us and saved us and called us with a holy calling [a calling that leads to a consecrated life—a life set apart—a life of purpose], not because of our works [or because of any personal merit—we could do nothing to earn this], but because of His own purpose and grace [His amazing, undeserved favor] which was granted to us in Christ Jesus before the world began [eternal ages ago]).

As I grew older, I knew of God's grace and had even experienced it, but over the years, there were times where I had allowed complacency to build in my heart. I remember one occasion feeling completely worn down and the spiritual weight felt heavy, which was the blame I continued to cast on myself for the break up. During those earlier stages of when Alexi and I had just broken up, I came across a quote that brought light back into what I was facing. It reminded me of how gracious our Father is and how He had always been unchanging in my life. For me, coming across this quote was more than just a simple encouragement. It was extremely humbling, yet empowering to know that God in all of His glory and supremacy could notice me amongst a crowd full of people and yet in my messiness, He still wanted me.

> "What made me love Christ wasn't that all of a sudden I figured out how to do life. What made me love Christ is that when I was at my worst, when I was at my lowest point, when I absolutely could not clean myself up and there was nothing anybody could do with me, right at that moment, Christ said, "I'll take that one. That's the one I want." - Matt Chandler

There are plenty of reasons to love and appreciate His grace, but one of the many things that stand out to me is that His grace isn't just for a particular type of person, or it doesn't require someone to live by certain conditions before receiving it. Regardless of who you are and what you have done, His grace is for you; it's for everyone. I'm grateful that this is the case because it meant that His grace was available for me too, even when I felt less than deserving to receive it at all. The Bible tells us that grace is a gift and that we can't earn it, but it's freely given through the sacrifice of Jesus dying for us; for the atonement of our sins.

Ephesians 2:8 AMP
For it is by grace [God's remarkable compassion and favor drawing you to Christ] that you have been saved [actually delivered from judgment and given eternal life] through faith. And this [salvation] is not of yourselves [not through your own effort], but it is the [undeserved, gracious] gift of God;

Sometimes it can be tricky to wrap our minds around the concept of God's grace because we as people naturally put a hierarchy on different 'versions' of sin and compare it to what the least type of sin is, to what the worst type of sin is. God doesn't view us in this way. When we've messed up, He demonstrates His grace by still choosing to pour out His loving-kindness onto us. We are accepted by Him, despite the pain we cause ourselves, others and even to Him, so when we really grasp the revelation of how gracious He is to us, then it has the powerful ability to completely transform us from the inside out.

Being able to experience God's grace has brought such a change in the way I view life and how I make choices along the way. This doesn't mean we live in perfection, but it does mean that we're able to walk in His freedom and view each day as an opportunity to further His Kingdom, while showing others that they too can experience the gift of grace. So, what is it that God's grace teaches us?

Titus 2:11-12 AMP
For the [remarkable, undeserved] grace of God that brings salvation has appeared to all men. It teaches us to reject ungodliness and worldly (immoral) desires, and to live sensible, upright, and godly lives [lives with a purpose that reflect spiritual maturity] in this present age.

Looking back on the journey God has taken me on, I've found so much peace in knowing that I don't have to measure up to receive grace because as The Bible writes time and time again, we are given it *freely*. Actually experiencing the grace of God is what propels us to live out a Godly and righteous life. Scott J Shifferd's article on the teaching of God's grace words it in a way that demonstrates how it affects us ongoing:

'The Christian must see God's grace as more than salvation from past sins, but also a deliverance from coming temptations. Christ forgives believers from past sins to keep them from future sins. Christians must see the extent of personal sins, and the loving grace that forgave a few sins is as great as the grace that forgives many sins.'[13]

---

13 [Online] Available at: https://godsbreath.net/2014/04/27/how-does-grace-teach/ [Accessed 17th December, 2019]

Experiencing God's grace helps us overcome past sins and the desire towards continuing to live *in* sin. Through His grace, we're able to break its power over us, recognise who we are in Christ and from that knowledge, choose righteousness over the impulsive ways of the world.

I used to think that because of grace I was able to get away with how I lived my life and the mistakes that were made along the way. This didn't necessarily mean I would use every reason to sin and that I would choose the wrong decisions just for the sake of it, but with this way of thinking, I found myself trying incredibly hard to avoid sinning, to the point that when I did fall into sin, it didn't have too much of an effect on me. The mentality I reverted to was something along the lines of: "Oh well, I tried as hard as I could, but good thing God's grace is able to cover me". I had to learn that 'living in unconditional grace is never an excuse to be irresponsible or hurtful.'[14] When I carefully review the choices I made and how I understood grace to be in those times of my life, I realise how works-driven, selfish and wrong my view on it was. Although I had accepted God, I didn't fully grasp what His saving grace really meant for me because I had still been performing by works. Grace

---

14   Dr. Henry Cloud & Dr. John Townsend, 'Boundaries In Marriage', *Yates & Yates*, p. 162

doesn't give us the license to sin and we certainly aren't given the right to abuse it. In fact, it's God's grace that allows us to realise our freedom from the bondage of sin, as well as the power it holds over us. Grace reiterates to us that sin no longer has dominion over our lives because we have been saved by it. When we choose to experience His grace in the way God intends for us, we are given the avenue towards living in freedom.

Every time I look back on my life and where God has taken me, I can't help but be grateful for what He's taught me and for what He continues to teach me. Every choice, every hurdle, every lesson and every prayer leads us to these glorious moments of feeling complete freedom in Him. I hope that as you too have walked on this journey, you have been able to experience the freedom and peace that He so willingly desires for us all to receive when choosing to lay everything down. Just know that every decision you make and every circumstance you face has a reason and through the posture of surrender, it's His desire to see you live out your greatest purpose. What a life it is to know our Father and to be wholly loved by Him. There truly is no greater love shown than the sacrifice of Jesus' life in place for us. That is the kind of honest surrender we should aspire to take part in every single day.

BIBLE SCRIPTURE REFERENCES

Bible scriptures marked AMP are taken from the AMP YouVersion of The Bible App

Bible scriptures marked ESV are taken from the ESV YouVersion of The Bible App

Bible scriptures marked TPT are taken from the TPT YouVersion of The Bible App

Bible scriptures marked NIV are taken from the NIV YouVersion of The Bible App

Bible scriptures marked NLT are taken from the NLT YouVersion of The Bible App

ABOUT THE AUTHOR

Angelie Patsianis is a Worship Leader at Influencers Church Australia. She is passionate about seeing people wholeheartedly give their life to Christ and live out their God-given purposes. She currently resides in Adelaide, South Australia with her husband, Alexi and is a cat mum to Boss and Bina. She is a lover of naps, reading, demolishing a perfectly cooked medium-rare steak and psychological thriller movies.

Her love for journaling was one of the catalysts towards writing her first book and through this, she endeavours to inspire those to find hope, peace and freedom in our Saviour.

www.ingramcontent.com/pod-product-compliance
Lightning Source LLC
Chambersburg PA
CBHW070158100426
42743CB00013B/2957